How to Trade Options

How to Trade Options

Copyright © 2023 by Brian Pezim, BSc, MBA

All rights are reserved. No part of this book may be reproduced or used in any manner without the expressed written permission of the copywrite owner except for the use of quotations in a book review.

First Paperback edition November 2023.

Paperback ISBN: 9798868471292.
Available in eBook.

Book cover design by Bear Bull Traders design team.
Layout and formatting by Nelly Murariu at PixBeeDesign.com.

How to Trade Options

A Complete Guide to Trading Options, Option Strategies and Risk Management

© **Brian Pezim, BSc, MBA**
Trader at Bear Bull Traders
www.bearbulltraders.com

DISCLAIMER

The author and www.BearBullTraders.com ("the Company"), including its employees, contractors, shareholders and affiliates, are NOT an investment advisory service, registered investment advisors or broker-dealers and does not undertake to advise clients on which securities they should buy or sell for themselves. It must be understood that a very high degree of risk is involved in trading securities. The Company, the author, the publisher and the affiliates of the Company assume no responsibility or liability for trading and investment results. Statements on the Company's website and in its publications are made as of the date stated and are subject to change without notice. It should not be assumed that the methods, techniques or indicators presented in these products will be profitable nor that they will not result in losses. In addition, the indicators, strategies, rules and all other features of the Company's products (collectively, "the Information") are provided for informational and educational purposes only and should not be construed as investment advice. Examples presented are for educational purposes only. Accordingly, readers should not rely solely on the Information in making any trades or investments. Rather, they should use the Information only as a starting point for doing additional independent research in order to allow them to form their own opinions regarding trading and investments. I suggest that traders and investors consult with their licensed financial advisors and tax advisors to determine the suitability of any investment.

Preface

I have been a long-term trader and investor in the stock market for a significant part of my life. I have traded stocks through the decades as the markets ebbed and flowed through many economic cycles.

In 2015, I was fortunate to meet Andrew Aziz. We both worked for a clean technology company, but as we worked together, we discovered a shared interest and passion for trading and education.

Several years later, Andrew wrote his first book on day trading and we began hosting a chatroom called Vancouver Traders. This small chatroom grew into a large trading community called Bearbulltraders.com. Today this large community is dedicated to teaching and helping others learn to trade and take control of their finances.

My interest in educating others led me to write my first book "How to Swing Trade" which was published in late 2018. I received positive feedback from readers so I subsequently wrote a second book, "Profiting as an Active Trader", with the same educational purposes in mind. It has been very heartening to read emails from people expressing not only their gratitude for the knowledge I shared in those two publications, but also explaining how that information has helped them with their own investment journey.

Seeing a lot of interest in options trading within our community, I decided to write this third volume. It is intended to give the reader a good understanding of how options work, the risks and rewards in trading options, and some trading strategies that can be used to execute profitable trades.

I truly hope that as you study the pages that follow, you will gain some useful insights into investing and trading in the options market. My additional hope is that "How to Trade Options" will have a beneficial impact on traders and investors, similar to that of my other two books.

Table of Contents

Chapter 1 Introduction 1

Chapter 2 Options Trading—The Basics 5
Option Ownership 5
Call Options 6
Put Options 9
Option Quotes 12
Buying and Selling Options 14
    Pricing of Options 14
    Process of Buying and Selling Options 15
    Account Requirements 15
Chapter Summary 16

Chapter 3 Volatility 19
Historical 20
Implied Volatility 21
Chapter Summary 24

Chapter 4 Options Versus Stocks 25
Going Long or Short 25
Margin Requirements 27
Exposure to Unexpected Risk 28
Trade Timing 29
Dividends 29
Chapter Summary 30

Chapter 5 Why Trade Options — 31
Leverage — 31
Hedging — 32
Additional Revenue — 33
Risks in Trading Options — 34
Chapter Summary — 36

Chapter 6 Options and the Greeks — 39
Delta — 39
Gamma — 43
Theta — 44
Greeks Takeaway — 47
Chapter Summary — 47

Chapter 7 The Gamma Squeeze — 49
What is a Gamma Squeeze — 49
Triggers for a Gamma Squeeze — 50
Effect of the Gamma Squeeze — 51
Strategies for Managing and Trading Gamma Squeezes — 52
Conclusions — 52
Chapter Summary — 53

Chapter 8 Options Expiry Dates — 55
Daily Options — 55
Weekly Options — 56
Long-term Options — 57
Chapter Summary — 58

Chapter 9 Purchasing and Selling Options — 61
Purchasing Options – Put or Call — 61
Selling Options – Put or Call — 67
Chapter Summary — 70

Chapter 10 Vertical Spreads — 73
Buying Vertical Spreads – Put or Call — 73
Selling Vertical Spreads – Puts and Calls — 82
Chapter Summary — 84

Chapter 11 Covered Calls and Puts — 87
Chapter Summary — 92

Chapter 12 Protecting Positions — 93
Purchasing a Put or Call — 93
Risk Reversals — 96
Protection Summary — 100
Chapter Summary — 101

Chapter 13 Straddles and Strangles — 103
Straddles — 104
Strangle — 107
Straddles Versus Strangles — 109
Straddles and Strangles Short Plays — 110
Chapter Summary — 113

Chapter 14 Stock Replacement Strategy — 115
Stock Replacement — 115
Risk Reversal Revisited — 118
Chapter Summary — 119

Chapter 15 Earnings Plays — 121
Pre-earnings — 121
Post-earnings — 126
Chapter Summary — 131

Chapter 16 Day Trading Using Options — 133
Building Experience and a Trade Book — 133

Leverage	135
Complexity of Options	137
Chapter Summary	138

Chapter 17 Unusual Options Activity — 141
Chapter Summary — 146

Chapter 18 Maximum Pain — 147
Chapter Summary — 149

Chapter 19 Triple Witching — 151
Chapter Summary — 152

Chapter 20 Risk Management — 153
Assessing Risk and Reward	154
Setting Stops and Targets	154
Managing Trade Size	156
Diversifying Your Holdings	158
Chapter Summary	160

Chapter 21 Journaling Your Trades — 161
Chapter Summary — 163

Chapter 22 Final Thoughts — 165

CHAPTER 1

Introduction

Those of you who are members of the Bear Bull Traders community know that besides being an active day trader, I manage a portion of my finances utilizing swing and position trading strategies. In managing my finances, I often use options which lend themselves well to all types of trading styles.

I strongly recommend that if you want to start trading options, you should already have a solid understanding of the stock market and how to trade equities. This book is not going to provide you with in-depth knowledge on the markets. This extensive amount of information is presented in my previous books "How to Swing Trade" and "Profiting as an Active Trader". Furthermore, if you intend on using options for day trading, then prerequisite reading would be "How to Day Trade for a Living" by Andrew Aziz.

In this book I start out providing some basic information about options and why you might consider incorporating them into your trading tool box. Traders and investors that already have a good understanding of how options work, how they are priced, and how they compare to stocks may want to skim the first 5 chapters.

In chapter 6, I explain what is referred to by options traders as the "Greeks" which includes delta, theta and gamma. The values for each of these Greeks are derived from calculations, and they can help the options trader determine the way options prices will react to a shifting market and underlying security conditions.

Chapter 7 covers a phenomenon called the gamma squeeze. After discussing the Greeks in the previous chapter, I explain how this squeeze can have a very powerful impact on the pricing of both the options and the underlying security.

When trading options a trader or investor has a lot more to consider compared to trading a stock. In chapter 8 I discuss the various expiry timeframes and how they may better fit into one particular trading style compared to another.

After getting a good understanding of how options work and are priced, in the chapter 9, I examine two basic and relatively straightforward directional trading strategies. These methods include buying puts and calls, and selling puts and calls.

In chapter 10, building on the previous chapter, I follow up with an explanation on how you can lower the cost of making directional bets using options. This strategy is referred to as a vertical spread, with two potential trade setups that can be implemented. I discuss both the pros and cons of using this type of options trade setup, and present some example trades for your consideration.

The next options strategy that I highlight in chapter 11 is known as a covered call (or put). The reference to "covered" means that you already have the underlying security in your portfolio. This is a strategy you could employ to collect some extra capital for your account while you continue to hold the existing security.

Chapter 12 presents some options strategies that can be used to protect profits on your existing security holdings. Many hedge funds and large portfolio managers use this technic to preserve their gains while maintaining their existing positions, because their large holdings are not as easy to get in and out of in a hurry.

In the following chapter I discuss several more advanced options strategies called straddles and strangles. These strategies are often used prior to a possible value changing event, such as an earnings release. When implementing these more complex trades it is important to have a good understanding of what your positions will do under different conditions.

Another one of the most straight-forward options strategies that can be used is referred to as a stock replacement play. It involves using options to take a position in an underlying security instead of purchasing that same security. This is detailed in chapter 14.

In chapter 15 I discuss earnings plays. Earnings releases represent a very good opportunity to use options to make a profit. This is because the implied volatility is usually elevated due to a possible value changing event for the company. There are two basic approaches to trading around earnings releases; taking a position before or after the event. The pros and cons of both approaches will be presented.

Options can be used in a variety of ways which include using them as a day trading vehicle. Chapter 16 highlights how the leverage that is inherent in options can magnify potential gains, compared to buying or selling stocks. I also point out the need to actively manage those trades to prevent outsized losses.

Chapter 17 discusses how some traders will watch for unusual options activity as an indicator of future moves in the price of an underlying stock and the associated options. Unusual activity can happen for a number of different reasons, so traders need to be aware that this is not always a reliable indicator.

Another unique options indicator is based on the principal of max pain. Many options are sold by market makers; therefore, it is in their best interest to see as many as possible expire worthless so the fund can keep the money. Max pain is covered in chapter 18.

Triple witching is an event that happens once a quarter. Although it does not necessarily represent a trading opportunity for retail traders, you should be aware of this phenomenon and how it can impact the options market. This topic is presented in chapter 19.

Whether you are trading stocks or options, for me, risk management is one of the most important aspects of trading and managing money. I covered this topic in my previous books, but it is always worth reviewing and reinforcing, which I have done in chapter 20. Never forget that preserving your capital is the most crucial thing you can do as a trader or investor.

Chapter 21 explores journaling. A trade journal will solidify your trading plan by documenting where you entered each trade that you took, and most importantly, where you stopped out if the trade did not go as you had expected. This is critical in managing your capital and surviving to trade another day.

Chapter 22 wraps up this guide with some final thoughts for you to ponder and reflect on. As I mentioned in my previous books, you must appreciate and always keep in mind that trading is not a method to "get rich quick". Novice traders are led to believe it is as simple as buying low and selling high. It sounds deceptively uncomplicated, but it is not.

For your convenience, at the end of each chapter I have provided a short summary of what was covered in point form. Veteran traders can use these synopses to check whether or not they already have an understanding of the skills and instruction contained in that particular chapter. Traders "in training" will be able to use these summaries as both a review exercise after working through a chapter, and for future reference when they are searching for a succinct encapsulation of a specific aspect of trading or investing.

My hope is that you can use this material to identify and execute profitable options trades, while being aware that you need to carefully manage the capital that you are putting at risk. I further hope that this book will benefit a broad audience, from the fledgling trader, aiming to make their initial options trade, to the more seasoned trader looking to expand their strategies and/or trading style.

CHAPTER 2

Options Trading— The Basics

In this first chapter I will cover everything you need to know about an option. For those already familiar with options, this will be a chapter you can breeze through before moving on to more unfamiliar options topics. The following material will be covered in this chapter:

» Option Ownership
» Call options
» Put options
» Option quotes
» Buying and selling options

You can consider this chapter a lesson on options basics. Subsequent chapters will explain different trading strategies that can be used in both trending and stagnating markets.

Option Ownership

When you purchase the stock of a company, you are essentially becoming a partial owner of that business. A stockholder is said to hold an equity position in the company. However, as an equity holder you are likely one of millions of other stockholders, so you have no influence on the enterprise even though you own a very small portion of it.

Now let's compare company stock to an option. An option is defined as a contract between a buyer and a seller for a specific period of time.

It is really nothing more than a binding agreement between two parties that can be bought and sold up to the expiry date of the agreement. The trader of an option does not own equity in the company. Instead, they own a right to buy or sell that equity.

The Chicago Mercantile Exchange (CME) facilitates the purchase and sale of these agreements by creating and maintaining a market and trading platform for them. Individuals and institutions act as either buyers or sellers of these agreements.

An option contract has four separate components:

1. a stock or security that an option contract is based on,
2. an expiration date,
3. an expiration price (commonly known as a strike price),
4. a choice of either a call or a put.

There are two primary options that you as a trader can buy or sell: a call option or a put option. In the following sections, I will discuss these two types of options and how they are traded.

Call Options

I will begin by outlining what a call option is, since most traders and investors, regardless of their experience, find them a little easier to understand than put options. When buying a call option (whether it be on a stock, an index, or an ETF), you are hoping that the security moves to the upside as quickly as possible. A purchaser of a call option is deemed to be long the position.

Do note that buying a call option on a security, to bet that its price will continue to rise, is not akin to simply buying the security because it is increasing in price. You are not buying the security. You are buying a call option on it. Many traders do not fully grasp how these options products work. This lack of comprehension can lead to losses if they are not used correctly. First and foremost, as an options trader you

Options Trading—The Basics

need to realize that the value of an option deteriorates over time. I will provide some commentary on this issue of deterioration in the pages to come.

In the case of a call option, the buyer of a call is purchasing the right to buy the underlying stock or security on or before a particular date and at a specific price. Figure 2.1 shows an example of an Apple Inc. (AAPL) option quote on March 30th, 2021. On this date, with AAPL trading at a bit under $120.00, you could have purchased a $120.00 call option for $0.90 (the "Ask" figure in the 4th column on the left-hand side). Be aware that 1 call option represents 100 shares and so the purchase cost of this call will be $90.00 ($0.90 times 100). For this trade to be profitable, AAPL must rise in price above the $120.90 level ($120.00 strike price plus the $0.90 paid for the call) prior to the expiry date of April 1st, 2021.

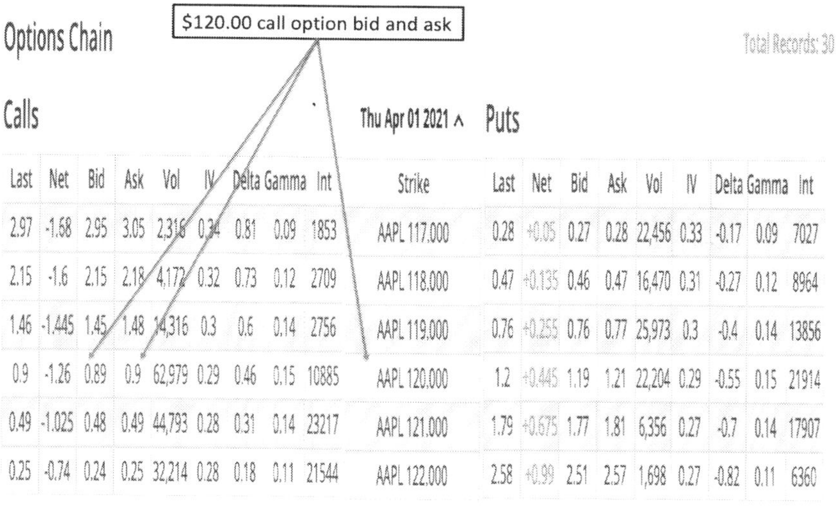

Options Chain — $120.00 call option bid and ask — Total Records: 30

Calls — Thu Apr 01 2021 ∧ — **Puts**

Last	Net	Bid	Ask	Vol	IV	Delta	Gamma	Int	Strike	Last	Net	Bid	Ask	Vol	IV	Delta	Gamma	Int
2.97	-1.58	2.95	3.05	2,316	0.34	0.81	0.09	1853	AAPL 117.000	0.28	+0.05	0.27	0.28	22,456	0.33	-0.17	0.09	7027
2.15	-1.6	2.15	2.18	4,172	0.32	0.73	0.12	2709	AAPL 118.000	0.47	+0.135	0.46	0.47	16,470	0.31	-0.27	0.12	8964
1.46	-1.445	1.45	1.48	14,316	0.3	0.6	0.14	2756	AAPL 119.000	0.76	+0.255	0.76	0.77	25,973	0.3	-0.4	0.14	13856
0.9	-1.26	0.89	0.9	62,979	0.29	0.46	0.15	10885	AAPL 120.000	1.2	+0.445	1.19	1.21	22,204	0.29	-0.55	0.15	21914
0.49	-1.025	0.48	0.49	44,793	0.28	0.31	0.14	23217	AAPL 121.000	1.79	+0.675	1.77	1.81	6,356	0.27	-0.7	0.14	17907
0.25	-0.74	0.24	0.25	32,214	0.28	0.18	0.11	21544	AAPL 122.000	2.58	+0.99	2.51	2.57	1,698	0.27	-0.82	0.11	6360

Figure 2.1 - Screenshot of a quotation for AAPL calls and puts expiring on April 1st, 2021 (courtesy of Cboe Global Markets, Inc.).

You can profit in 2 different ways on this trade. Given that an option contract can be bought and sold multiple times in advance of its expiry date, you could resell the option at a higher price to another buyer. To make a short-term profit on this trade, the stock price of AAPL would need to go up. Therefore, before it expires, you can take advantage of a corresponding price gain in the option. You may not want to acquire the security at all, so you could just sell the option up to the final minutes of the day that it is expiring, locking in any increase in the original purchase price of the option.

Secondly, you can profit by holding the option until it expires (if the stock is trading above the strike price). In this instance, you will obtain the underlying security at the strike price because the option contract has accorded you that right. You will be required to pay the full price for the stock. Using this example of AAPL, you would be obligated to purchase the shares at $120.00. For 1 call option the cost of the purchase would be $12,000.00 (100 shares per call option times $120.00). Obviously as a trader you would be quite happy in this situation if, at the expiry of your call option, the shares were trading at $125.00 per share.

On the other side of the transaction, the seller of the call option is initially collecting money from the purchaser and hoping that either the call will be worthless when it expires, or that they can buy it back at a lower price in the future. Once the call reaches the expiry date, it is exercised if it is in the money (which I will explain in a couple of pages), or if it is of no value it is left to die by the call purchaser. If it does die worthless, so to speak, the call option seller keeps the money paid by the purchaser.

Returning to Figure 2.1 and AAPL, if the price of AAPL is $115.00 on the expiry date, the contract to purchase the shares at $120.00 is worthless since you can go to the marketplace and buy AAPL at the lower price. If, however, AAPL is trading at $125.00, then the call option holder will be delighted to sell their call at a higher price or exercise their right to buy the stock at the lower price of $120.00 (compared to the $125.00 they would have to pay in the market).

The screenshot in Figure 2.1 displays 6 strike prices and 1 expiry date for AAPL. In reality, the opportunities to trade calls in AAPL were much broader. The table shows only a fraction of the option trading possibilities for March 30th, 2021. There were additional strike prices available further away from what was that day's current stock price.

Put Options

I want to now examine put options, which are essentially the opposite of call options. Purchasing a put option allows you to take a position on a stock or security that you believe is going to fall in price. Just like a call option, a put option is a contract between a buyer and a seller, but the buyer of the option is purchasing the right to sell the underlying security to the seller of the option. In the case of a put option the buyer is considered to be short the position.

For example, let's say that Microsoft Corporation (MSFT) is trading at $232.00 per share. If you believe that the stock of MSFT is about to drop below $230.00 before an option expiry date on April 1st, 2021, you could consider buying a $230.00 put option for $0.81 (the "Ask" figure in the 4th column on the right-hand side of Figure 2.2). This would give you the right to sell shares of MSFT at $230.00. The purchase of this put would cost you $81.00 ($0.81 times 100 shares). This put will become more valuable as the MSFT share price falls and approaches your $230.00 level prior to its expiry date.

If by chance some bad news comes out regarding MSFT ahead of the expiry of your put option, and their price drops to $225.00 per share, then the value of your put option rises significantly. As the put holder you have a position similar to being "short the shares", and therefore you can make money as the security price continues to decrease. The seller of the put option is required to buy the shares from you at a price of $230.00, which is higher than their market price of $225.00.

How to Trade Options

Options Chain

Total Records: 30

Calls   Thu Apr 01 2021 ∧   **Puts**

$225.00 put option bid and ask

Last	Net	Bid	Ask	Vol	IV	Delta	Gamma	Int	Strike	Last	Net	Bid	Ask	Vol	IV	Delta	Gamma	Int
7	-3.15	6.85	8.35	107	0.02	1	0.03	383	MSFT 225.000	0.21	+0.01	0.12	0.21	1,815	0.3	-0.08	0.03	3364
4.45	-3.325	4.7	5.5	211	0.24	0.87	0.05	709	MSFT 227.500	0.36	+0.03	0.32	0.43	2,346	0.27	-0.16	0.05	2553
3.26	-2.265	2.79	3.25	3,192	0.21	0.74	0.09	1556	MSFT 230.000	0.94	+0.345	0.65	0.81	5,240	0.25	-0.31	0.08	6580
1.52	-1.905	1.4	1.6	9,472	0.21	0.48	0.11	2529	MSFT 232.500	2.06	+0.97	1.55	1.9	2,986	0.25	-0.52	0.09	3407
0.56	-1.295	0.52	0.6	15,475	0.21	0.23	0.08	8509	MSFT 235.000	3.5	+1.435	2.98	3.9	1,177	0.26	-0.73	0.07	4651
0.23	-0.625	0.2	0.25	4,643	0.23	0.1	0.04	6260	MSFT 237.500	5.6	+2.05	4.7	6.25	191	0.29	-0.85	0.05	1925

Figure 2.2 - Screenshot of a quotation for MSFT puts and calls expiring on April 1st, 2021 (courtesy of Cboe Global Markets, Inc.).

Once again, there are 2 ways for you to make money on this trade. As with calls, puts can be bought and sold (i.e., resold) at any time up to the expiry date of the option contract, permitting either party to exit the trade at any time in advance of the contract's expiry. Upon the sale of the option, you have no further obligation with respect to the option contract.

If you retain a profitable option trade through to its expiry date, you will be compelled to sell shares to the put seller at the contract price. This means that you may now be short the shares unless you are holding shares in your account to cover the sale.

As you read along in this book, I will explain the time value of options and why it is often better for you to exit a position prior to the expiry of the contract. I will also outline why investors might want to hold options on the securities that they presently own.

Before detailing what an options quote is comprised of, I want to discuss three terms that you need to be familiar with: at the money (ATM), in the money (ITM), and out of the money (OTM). These three expressions refer to the relationship between the strike price of the option you are considering in comparison to the current price of the security.

For example, if AAPL stock is trading at $120.00 and you are holding a $115.00 call, then that call is described as being ITM. You are in the money, so to speak. Your call (the contract with the right to buy) has inherent value because the strike price is $5.00 below the present price.

But what happens if AAPL falls to $115.00 the next day? Your $115.00 call is then ATM. You are at the money. The call strike price equals the underlying security price.

The last scenario is when AAPL drops beneath $115.00 (let's say to $112.00). The $115.00 call is OTM. You are out of the money. The call strike price is above the current market price of AAPL. No rational investor would exercise their call at the $115.00 price when they can buy shares on the market at $112.00.

The same terminology applies to puts if the situation is reversed. A $145.00 put holder is ITM if the stock price of AAPL is $142.00 because they hold the rights to sell their shares at $145.00. On the other hand, a $145.00 AAPL put holder is OTM if the stock is trading at $150.00. No investor will exercise a right to sell AAPL at $145.00 when they can sell it on the market at $150.00

I hope these comments have left you with a solid understanding of calls and puts. In the following section I want to review the elements of an option quote.

Option Quotes

As I mentioned above, option contracts have four specific components:

1. the underlying stock or security that the contract is based on and you want to trade,
2. an expiration date,
3. an expiration price (strike price),
4. a choice of either a call or a put.

Figure 2.3 shows a typical option quote that you will find on the Cboe Global Markets, Inc. website. This particular option quote is for Square Inc. (SQ), the underlying security which is the first required component in an option quote. You will also find the date of expiry, which is the second option quote requirement. In this case, the date is April 30th, 2021. It is up to you to decide whether you want a longer date to expiry or a shorter date.

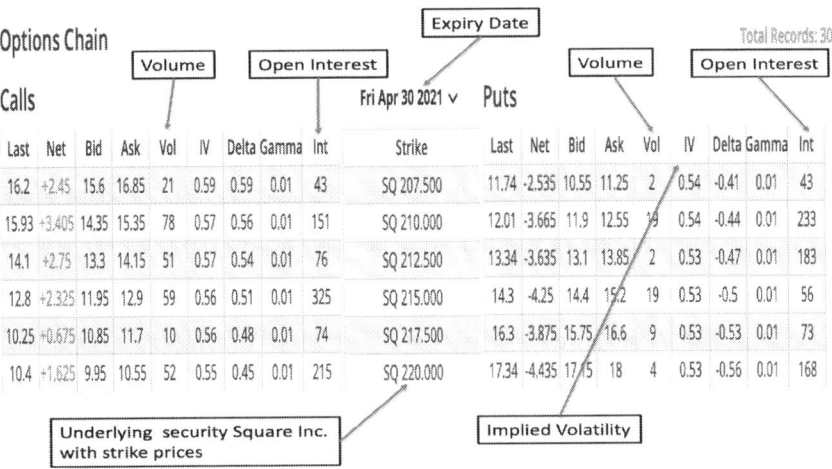

Figure 2.3 – Screenshot of an option quotation for SQ expiring on April 30th, 2021 (courtesy of Cboe Global Markets, Inc.).

Options Trading—The Basics

There are a number of items to note in this SQ option table. First off, the table represents 1 specific expiry date. Each expiry date will have its own table that will contain different strike prices (located in the middle of the table). The associated current bid and ask for each strike price is also shown for both the calls and the puts.

The available option expiry dates can vary depending on the underlying security. For instance, a very actively traded option such as the SPY have expiry dates for every trading day. With SQ and many other actively traded securities, there are option contracts available to trade which expire every Friday of the year (except when Friday is a market holiday). All optionable securities have monthly options that expire on the third Friday of the month.

As an options trader, you can use quarterly options or even longer time frames. The latter are referred to as Long-Term Equity Anticipation Securities (LEAPS). LEAPS options would be used to make a very long-term bet on a company or other security, and usually expire at least 1 year from the date of purchase.

I consider myself more of a short-term trader and so I rarely use LEAPS options. However, as of the writing of this book, I am holding some Ford LEAPS options that are about 1 year to expiry. I believe that Ford's introduction of their new electric vehicles is promising from the perspective of stock appreciation, but I also believe it will take time for their positive commitment to electric vehicles to be reflected in the price of their stock.

Two other items in the above option quotation that I want to briefly focus on are the volume and open interest columns. The volume number indicates how many contracts were opened on the current trading day. The open interest number tells you how many contracts exist at present between buyers and sellers. Higher levels of volume and open interest mean that the options are being more actively traded. and that is a good sign for active option traders. More participants translates into more liquidity, and that results in a smaller "spread" between the bid and the ask prices.

Buying and Selling Options

Now that I have reviewed the basics of options, let's examine the following topics related to the buying and selling of options:

- » Pricing of options
- » The process of buying and selling options
- » The account requirements

Pricing of Options

There are seven variables that determine the price of an option:

1. the strike price,
2. the current price of the underlying security,
3. the time left until the expiration of the option,
4. whether it is a call or put option,
5. the risk-free interest rate – usually the yield on a Treasury bill,
6. whether dividends are being paid on the underlying security during the options contract,
7. implied volatility.

Six of these variables are known. The strike price is the option contract price you are looking at in comparison to the current price of the underlying asset. The time to expiration is another choice you make based on the tables with different option expiry dates. The choice of a call or put depends on whether you are bearish or bullish combined with the strategy you want to employ. Lastly, the Treasury bill interest rate and whether a dividend is due to be paid is all easily researched.

The seventh variable, implied volatility, is the unknown variable. This volatility variable is only an estimate, and it can even vary throughout the course of a trading day. For this reason, it is one of the most important factors to influence the price of an option. Due to the importance that implied volatility plays with option pricing and strategies, I will be discussing this topic separately in the next chapter.

Process of Buying and Selling Options

Buying options is practically as simple as buying stocks. From a process perspective it is purely point and click. Nevertheless, unlike stocks, with options you will have several additional decisions to make aside from the underlying security selection.

As discussed in the previous sections, with options you must decide on the strike price you want to buy or sell at, and how much time you want available to be able to hold the option before it expires. These 2 added decisions are dependent on numerous factors, including the purpose for taking the option trade in the first place. I will outline the 3 main reasons for trading options shortly.

The strike price and expiry date you choose should be based primarily on the fundamental and technical analysis of the security that you will have conducted. For those that have a limited knowledge on this analysis, I strongly suggest you read one of my previous books (How to Swing Trade or Profiting as an Active Trader) to gain insight on developing a trade plan. How to put all of this information together to make a potentially profitable trade will be set forth in the coming chapters.

Account Requirements

The account requirements for options trading are quite straightforward. For most brokers you will need to complete some forms that acknowledge you understand the risks in trading options, and that you will not hold the broker liable for any possible losses. Brokers make it very easy for you to trade options, so it is up to you to educate yourself thoroughly prior to jumping into this arena.

Speaking of arenas, imagine for a moment that you are living in ancient Rome. You do not desire to be a trader, though you want to be a gladiator, and you are seeking all the fame and fortune that career entails. Would you just go shopping at an ancient Roman Walmart and buy a sword, shield, armor, and then head down to the Colosseum?

Of course not. As a gladiator hopeful, you are aware that you will be stepping into an arena filled with professional and seasoned fighters. These pros will slice and dice you in a heartbeat.

The options and stock markets are exactly the same. Strictly opening an account is not enough. You might get lucky on 1 or 2 trades, but presumably you are in this for the long run. You must study and train to be a professional and successful gladiator in the options markets.

CHAPTER SUMMARY

You can consider this chapter a lesson on options basics. The following topics were covered:

- » An option is a contract between a buyer and a seller for a specific period of time. The buyer of an option does not own equity in a security. Instead, they own a right to buy or sell that security.
- » There are 2 basic option types: a call option and a put option
- » When buying a call option (whether it be on a stock, an index, or an ETF), you are hoping that the security moves to the upside as quickly as possible.
- » When buying a put option (whether it be on a stock, an index, or an ETF), you are hoping that the security moves downward in price as quickly as possible.
- » Option contracts have four specific components: the underlying stock or security that the contract is based on and you want to trade, an expiration date, a strike price, and it is either a "call" or a "put".
- » There are seven variables that determine the price of an option: the strike price you are considering, the current price of the underlying security, the time left until the expiration of the option, whether it is a call or put option, the risk-free interest rate (usually

Options Trading—The Basics

the yield on a Treasury bill), whether dividends are being paid on the underlying security during the options contract, and the implied volatility.

» The implied volatility is the only variable that is somewhat subjective and constantly changing. It is determined by the buyers and sellers in the market.

» Buying and selling options is similar to buying and selling stocks, however there are a few more purchase decisions to be made such as strike price and date to expiry.

» Accounts need to be authorized and approved by your broker to buy and sell options.

CHAPTER 3

Volatility

As we discussed in the previous chapter, the pricing of an option is based on seven variables. Six of these seven variables are known entities as follows:

1. the strike price,
2. the current price of the underlying security,
3. the time left until the expiration of the option,
4. whether it is a call or put option,
5. the risk-free interest rate – usually the yield on a Treasury bill,
6. whether dividends are being paid on the underlying security during the options contract.

The seventh variable, which is not readily defined, is volatility. This volatility variable is only an estimate and it can change constantly, even throughout the course of a trading day. For this reason, it is one of the most important factors to influence the price of an option.

Since the other six inputs to an option's price are known and volatility is strictly an approximation, traders will have differing opinions about the value to assign to volatility. Therefore, trading volatility is an integral part of the strategies used by options traders.

First off, you should be aware that there are two measures of volatility:

1. Historical (also referred to as Realized)
2. Implied

How to Trade Options

I will discuss each separately below.

Historical

Historical volatility (HV) is a backward-looking measure over a period of time, such as the past month or year. HV is merely a calculation so there is no guesswork or estimation involved in coming up with this value. The computation provides you with an amount that the security has deviated from its average price, over a specific time frame.

For example, let's look at the historical deviation that has occurred with the AAPL share price over the last 10 years. Figure 3.1 shows how much the AAPL stock price deviated from its average price for each of the years. Looking at the chart you can see a big spike in 2020. This was a result of the Covid lock-downs and subsequent temporary crash that happened in the markets. During 2020 the AAPL share price varied almost 22% from its average over that period. This is a very high level of volatility for AAPL based on its prior trading history.

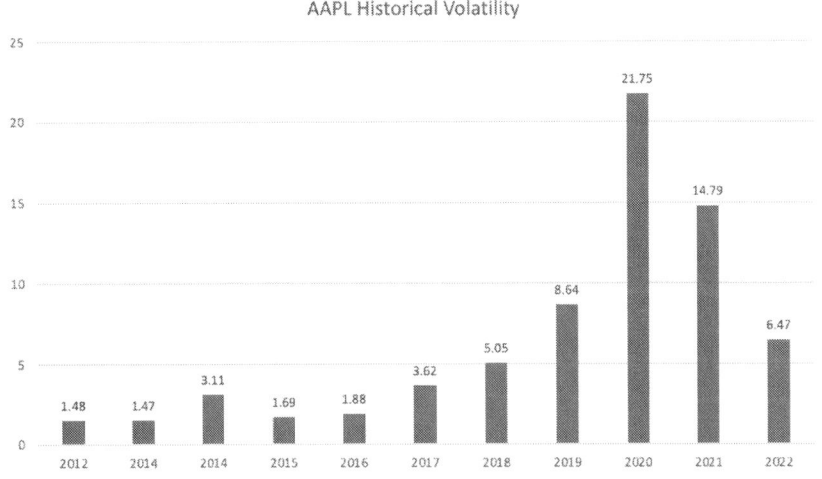

Figure 3.1 A chart showing the historical annual volatility of AAPL and illustrating how it can change year-over-year based on current events.

While the study of historical volatility can give you a hint or indication of volatility value expectations in the future, this value is based on past moves which may not be indicative of future price variations. This is why implied volatility is more relevant for options traders.

Implied Volatility

In comparison to historical volatility, implied volatility (IV) is an estimate of the volatility of the underlying security that is implied by the current options prices. Buyers and sellers in the market are essentially determining this IV through the free market forces of supply and demand.

Accordingly, IV is more relevant than historical volatility for the pricing of options because it is a forward-looking measure. The IV values listed in most options tables are calculated using a formula called the Black-Scholes model. Fortunately for traders, the IV is computed for you by most options quote providers, as shown in each of the figures in the previous chapter.

All else being equal, an elevated level of IV will result in higher options prices, while a depressed level of IV will lead to lower options prices. For example, volatility typically spikes around the time a company reports earnings. Therefore, the IV priced in by traders for a company's options at earnings season will generally be significantly higher than their approximations of volatility during "calmer and uneventful" times.

One of the main take-aways we can learn from the level of IV is when to be a buyer of options and when it is better to be a seller. Generally speaking, most options traders agree that when IV is relatively low, it is a better strategy to buy options, and when IV is high it is better to be a seller. We will explore this concept later in the book.

While we are on the topic of IV, lets discuss a particular measure of market IV referred to as the VIX. This is one of the gauges that many traders and investors watch as a forward-looking indicator for the market. The VIX value measures how much the market participants believe the S&P 500 index options will change over the coming year. The formula used to generate this value is based on calculations that look at the difference between the put and call options prices.

As we already discussed, options prices are based on trader's and investor's market volatility expectations between the current date and expiry date of the options. When the VIX is trending down or at a low level (typically below 20) the market is usually in a bull mode. When the VIX starts to spike higher, it usually means that markets are either selling off or are about to sell off.

The old adage "bulls take the stairs up and bears take the window down" applies to the VIX. Generally speaking, during bull markets the indexes and most stocks move higher at a slow and measured pace. When sell-offs happen the moves tend to be more exaggerated, therefore we get a higher level of volatility and a higher VIX.

Higher levels of volatility mean that traders are expecting larger price moves of a stock or index (up or down). This is why options become more expensive during more volatile markets. The VIX is often referred to as the "fear gauge" because it goes up during uncertain market conditions or when markets sell off.

Figure 3.2 is a chart of the VIX. You can see that the VIX is very low and has even been heading lower. Market participants clearly saw no fear of an imminent sell-off in the indexes when this chart was generated.

You cannot trade the VIX like you would a stock, however sophisticated investors can trade options or futures on the VIX. For the less sophisticated retail trader there are a number of products such as exchange-traded funds (ETF) and exchange-traded notes (ETN) that enable you to trade volatility.

Volatility

Figure 3.2 A chart of the VIX compared to the performance of SPX. As the market moves higher, the VIX continues to drop (chart courtesy of StockCharts.com).

The obvious question is, "how can you use this information to your advantage when trading options. One of the fundamental principles of investing is to buy low and sell high. This adage can also be applied to trading options. As mentioned above, when IV is low, options traders will often buy options due to the lower cost. Alternatively, when IV is high, traders will often sell options to take advantage of the higher prices.

Based on the VIX chart in Figure 3.2, in early March when the VIX was elevated, it may have been more profitable to be the seller of options. Several months later in June it may have been more lucrative to buy options with the VIX very low.

We will discuss a number of different strategies for buying and selling options under different IV conditions later in the book. Just remember, as with all indicators, none are perfect or 100% reliable as a predictor of future volatility and risk.

CHAPTER SUMMARY

In chapter 3 we explored the meaning of volatility as it applies to options. The main points of the chapter are as follows:

» There are two types of volatility. One is referred to as historical volatility and the other is called implied volatility.

» Historical volatility (also called realized volatility) is a backward-looking number that is calculated over a defined period of time. It is a value that measures how much a security price has deviated from its average price. Because it is backward-looking, it is of less value compared to the implied number.

» In comparison to historical volatility, implied volatility (IV) is an estimate of the volatility of the underlying security that is implied by the current option price.

» IV is determined through the free market forces of supply and demand generated by traders. The value of IV is derived using a calculation developed by Black-Scholes.

» All else being equal, an elevated level of IV will result in a higher option price, while a depressed level of IV will lead to a lower option price.

» Generally speaking, when IV is relatively low it is often a better strategy to buy options, and when IV is high it is often better to be a seller.

» A particular measure of market IV is referred to as the VIX. When the VIX is trending down or at a low level (typically below 20) the market is usually in a bull mode.

» Higher levels of volatility mean that traders are expecting larger price moves of a stock or index (up or down). This is why options become more expensive during volatile markets.

CHAPTER 4

Options Versus Stocks

In this chapter, I will discuss the differences in trading options compared to stocks. Trading options has some distinct advantages over stock trading, however there are also some downsides that you need to be aware of. The rewards can be high but with an expectation of a higher reward comes a higher level of risk to your capital. The following topics will cover comparisons of the two trading vehicles:

- » Going long or short
- » Margin requirements
- » Exposure to unexpected risk
- » Trade timing
- » Dividends

In each of the sections I will discuss how these differences can work for you or against you.

Going Long or Short

As I discussed in the previous chapter, when you purchase the stock of a company you are essentially becoming a partial owner of that business. Alternatively, if you purchase an option based on the stock of a company, you are merely entering into a contractual agreement with another party for a specific period of time. As purchaser of an option, you do not own equity in the company. Instead, you own a right to buy or sell that equity.

As a trader or investor with capital to deploy in the market, you have a choice of purchasing the stock (if you are bullish) or take a long position with a call option on that stock (if there are options available to trade). If you have a negative view of the stock, you could consider selling the stock short or purchasing a put option. These are referred to as directional bets on the price of a stock.

However, what if you feel that the stock is stuck in a trading range and will likely remain there for some time to come? If you are correct, going long or short the shares will be "dead money", or in other words, capital that is not earning a return. With options you can make what are referred to as non-directional investments. Being the seller of a put option, a call option, or both allows you to collect money from the buyer. And if you are correct, you can keep that money when the options contracts expire or you chose to buy them back.

Under a different scenario, maybe you feel that the stock is going to make a big move one way or the other – you just do not know which way the move will be. This situation could occur in the case of an earnings release. You could buy both a put and a call option, simultaneously before the event, to capture a large move one way or the other. You would do this expecting that the gain seen in the one option will exceed the loss in value of the other option. With stocks you would never sell and buy a security simultaneously, because the positive move in one position will just cancel the negative move in the other position.

Selling puts and calls to capture non-directional moves in a security, or simultaneously buying puts and calls to capture large movements, are two scenarios where options have a distinct advantage over stock ownership. They give you the opportunity to capitalize on these unique situations should you decide to take these trades.

In summary, just like stocks, options allow you to take a long or short position in a stock based on your assessment of the future price direction of those shares. However, options also have the added advantage of allowing you to make non-directional bets on a share price, if you feel the stock will be trading within a price range for a period of time.

Margin Requirements

Trading options and options ownership have a clear advantage over stock ownership when it comes to capital and meeting margin requirements. Let's start with an example comparing the purchase of some AAPL shares versus buying call options. As of June 2023, purchasing 100 shares of AAPL at a current price of $180, it will cost $18,000. If you only have $12,000 cash in your account for this trade, your broker is happy to loan you $6,000 and charge interest on that loan.

Alternatively, if you thought AAPL had more juice to go higher, you could buy a $180 at the money call option, expiring in a few weeks for $300 ($3.00 per contract representing 100 shares). Now you only have use $300 in your account, with no interest expense, while having the opportunity to participate in a further stock price increase.

If you are buying a put or call option, the most you can lose is the money you paid for that option. The situation is very different if you are the seller of options contracts and particularly with no protection. This is referred to as naked option selling and it exposes you to a lot of risk. If you happen to make an incorrect bet on a stock, the loss you could experience may be many times the money you got for selling the option. For this reason, a broker will require you to have excess capital in your account in case your option selling trade becomes a loser.

There are ways of selling put and call options with limited loss protection. These strategies will be covered later in the book. Just be aware that buying put or call options can allow you to participate in stock moves, without incurring borrow costs or using all of your capital with one or two positions.

In conclusion, options give you the opportunity to participate in share price moves at a much lower cost compared to an outright purchase of the shares.

Exposure to Unexpected Risk

As a trader or investor in the market, you will always be exposed to the potential of unexpected events that impact your holdings negatively. It could be an announcement of a Securities and Exchange Commission (SEC) investigation into the practices of a company you hold shares in. It could be a lawsuit or the company doing a round of fund raising at a price below the current market price. If you are short a stock or a put holder, news of a richly priced buyout could drive the stock price much higher. Whatever the case, unexpected events do occur and you need to be mentally prepared for the day that it will happen to one of your holdings.

When negative events occur in a company you hold shares in long, the share price will drop. If you hold call options in that stock, then the price of those options will also suffer a loss as well. Depending on the time to expiry and strike price, the options could go to zero. The only good news in this scenario is that the most you can lose is what the option cost you to purchase. In comparison, the drop in the share price could be much higher and result in a more significant loss.

Being stuck holding stocks versus options through unexpected events can result in a better outcome, or a worse outcome, depending your option investment and the parameters of the options contract. In addition, if you consider yourself a long-term holder of the stock, being long the shares may allow you to ride out the pullback. With options, you may not have that luxury as the option contract may expire before the share price has a chance to recover.

The bottom line is that holding stocks or options do not protect you from the exposure to unexpected risk. Holding options long does give you the assurance that the most you can lose is the amount that you paid for the option. Just remember, being a seller of puts or calls through a big price moving event is a different situation that could cause losses much higher than the premium you collected.

Trade Timing

Recall that purchasing an option requires you to decide on a strike price and an expiry date for that contract. If you are making a directional bet on the stock, at the very least the price of the underlying security needs to move in favor of your strike price for the option value to increase. If you are correct in your bet, then the option price will increase as well.

However, if the share price moves in the opposite direction of where you expected it to go, or it does not move at all, then your options value will start to decay as the expiry date approaches. We will discuss the important topic of the price decay later in the book. You need to consider that the value of the options will eventually go to zero if it expires OTM.

Alternatively, the long-term stock holder has the luxury of waiting out the ups and the downs in share price. There is no expiry to the ownership of shares. In this regard, share ownership can provide some security in the knowledge that each day that passes is not resulting in a naturally decaying price that options would see.

Dividends

Dividends payment is a straight-forward topic when it comes to stocks versus holding options on the same underlying security. As a stock holder, you are entitled to any dividends that might be paid by the company. Dividends are a method used by companies to return profits to their shareholders.

As an options holder, you are not entitled to dividends. Remember that your options are merely a contract between a buyer and a seller regarding the security. You are not an equity holder and do not share in any profits.

CHAPTER SUMMARY

In this chapter I discussed the differences in owning options compared to stocks. A summary of the discussion follows:

- » As a stock or equity holder you are a partial owner of the company, albeit likely a very small holder on a percentage basis.
- » As an option holder, you have entered into a contractual agreement with another party to buy (a call) or sell (a put) of an underlying security by a defined date.
- » Options allow you to make directional bets on a stock if you believe the price is going to rise or fall, but also allows you to make non-directional bets if you think the price will remain relatively unchanged over a period of time.
- » Owning options on a stock versus owning the actual stock requires significantly less capital which can give you more "bang" for your buck.
- » Unexpected events can happen, and when they do it can be good or bad depending on the news and your current position. With options, the potential loss on negative news is always limited to the long positions of your options. Options value can go to zero, but the loss on a stock position can be significantly more.
- » Options have an expiry date. Stocks do not. The value of options decay as the expiry date draws closer, so you need to be aware of that when taking a position. If you pay $3.00 for a $100 call on a stock, and the stock does not move by expiry, your $300.00 is gone. If you bought the stock, you still own it at the same price with no loss.
- » Dividends are only paid to shareholders of a security. Options holders do not receive dividends.

CHAPTER 5
Why Trade Options

Now let's look at why you may prefer to use options contracts over owning the underlying stock or security. The reasons are summarized as follows:

- » Leverage
- » Hedging
- » Additional revenue

I will explain these three different opportunities for using options in detail below.

Leverage

Leverage essentially allows you to use your capital in a way that gets you a better return. For instance, let's assume Microsoft Corporation (MSFT) is trading at $225.00 per share and you sense it is going to rise in the near future. You could buy 100 shares of MSFT for $22,500.00. That is a fair amount of money for many people. Alternatively, you could buy a $230.00 call option on MSFT that expires in a week. This is a relatively short timeframe, but for this example let's assume you are expecting a quick price move. Let's say the cost of that call is about $3.00. Instead of spending $22,500.00 for 100 shares on a stock purchase, as a call option buyer you would pay $300.00 for the right to buy 100 shares.

If the price of MSFT shares starts to move up aggressively at the beginning of the 7-day period, getting closer to or above your $230.00 target, the call option will also move up aggressively in value. While your purchase of 100 shares will have increased by $500.00 (a respectable 2.22% on a $22,500.00 investment), as a call option buyer you would likely have seen the value of your call double to $6.00, depending on how fast the move was and how close the call is to its expiry date. This would have been a 100% gain compared to only 2.22% with the share purchase. You do need to recognize that as the expiry date approaches, if MSFT does not move up quickly as you had hoped and instead stays around $225.00, the option value will drop quickly while the value of the MSFT shareholding will remain unchanged.

The use of options to make a bet on the direction a security's price will move is a common strategy employed by some options traders. The small cost of the options, as opposed to buying the stock, can give you a much greater return on investment, but can also lead to a much higher percentage loss if you have misjudged the trend.

Hedging

Hedging is the equivalent of taking out an insurance policy on an existing position. Let's say you own 100 Meta Platforms, Inc. (META) shares with an original entry of $200.00 per share. Time has passed since you bought those shares, and the "old" Facebook is now trading at $250.00 per share, which is a very nice increase. You do not want to sell the shares because you believe there is a good chance that the stock price is going to keep moving up. However, you do not want your hard-earned gains in the stock to evaporate if some bad news comes out on META and the stock sells off.

To safeguard those gains rather than selling your META shares, you could purchase a put option at say $230.00, which as I discussed, is a right to sell the shares at a specific price. This put may expire

Why Trade Options

worthless if the shares do not drop in price, but if META does sell off steeply back to $200.00 per share, then you have the right to sell your shares at the $230.00 per share price.

These insurance-type strategies are often used by large investment firms as a way to protect gains on their holdings, which are much bigger in comparison to retail trader's accounts. Depending on market conditions these hedging trades can be expensive, and similar to insurance, may expire unused resulting in a loss of the funds invested. As a trader you will need to decide if this method is one you want to consider using as a means to shield your profits.

Additional Revenue

Options can also be used to create additional revenue on an existing holding. Let's use the same example from the previous section. You hold 100 shares of META. Your entry price was $200.00 and the current price is $250.00 per share. You could use that position to produce additional income by selling a call above the current price, using your existing holding as collateral.

In this case, you may look at your charts and surmise that $275.00 per share is a price that META would be unlikely to get to in the coming weeks. You could then sell a $275.00 call option and collect the proceeds from the buyer of that call. Perhaps this will generate about $500.00 for you (the call option price might be $5.00 on 1 call option of 100 shares). As the META shareholder, you are expecting that META will not get to $275.00 by the expiry date so that you can retain the extra $500.00 that you have brought in.

The downside of this "revenue generating strategy" occurs if the META shares unexpectedly go above the $275.00 per share strike price before the expiry date. Should that happen, you have two options:

1. You can allow the options to expire, which will force you to deliver (give up) the META shares you own to the option buyer (your broker will remove the shares from your account). It is

not the end of the world because you get to keep the $500.00 you received from selling the call, plus you benefited from the increase in share price (the rise from $250.00 to $275.00 per share). However, if the share price went to $300.00 you will have given up another $20.00 per share in profit ($275.00 plus the $5.00 call option less the $300.00 share price).

2. Alternatively, you can buy back the call at any time prior to its expiry so you are no longer obligated to return the shares. You may choose to do this if you feel strongly about holding onto the META shares for subsequent gains. You may end up taking a loss on the options part of the trade, but you will remain in the black on the META stock that you are holding. Do note that you have collected $5.00 for the call option, so if the option expires with the META share price under $280.00 you are still going to be profitable on the options trade as well. It is only when the price of META closes above the $280.00 per share level on expiry that the option sale becomes a loss.

Selling calls on an existing long position can be very effective in a market where stocks are trading in a range without trending in any particular direction. On the other hand, if you are short a position you can sell a put against that position. This strategy can be utilized with either long or short stock holdings. It is wise to first conduct some technical analysis and review previous levels of resistance and support on your charts. You will find that these levels are generally solid areas from which to pick strike prices for your options call and put sales.

Risks in Trading Options

There are additional risks to trading options over stocks that you should be well aware of. Foremost, leverage in trades works both ways. An options trade that does not go in your favor is apt to lose more money on a percentage basis, in the same fashion that I

Why Trade Options

described how options can magnify your gains. Never forget, a knife cuts both ways.

Secondly, options have an expiry date. Intrinsic in this expiry date is the time value of the option. If you purchase an option that will expire in 3 months, there is a significant amount of time for the security to move closer to the strike price that you are hoping for. However, as the expiry date approaches, and if the stock is not making progress toward the strike price, logic would tell you that the odds are becoming less and less likely for it to finish ITM (in the money). As the clock ticks down to the expiry date, so does the time value inherent in the price of the option.

In these circumstances, your investment in the options slowly erodes away. If you were to hold the position right to its expiry date and it ended up OTM (out of the money), all your investment in the options would be gone. In comparison, if you owned the stock and not the options, at the conclusion of the 3 months you would continue to own the stock.

As an example, if you bought META at $275.00 per share and it did not change in price for a month, you would still own shares of META 30 days later. If instead you purchased a $275.00 call for, say $4.00, and the stock stayed at $275.00 until its expiry, the $400.00 paid for the call option would be lost ($4.00 times 1 option contract for 100 shares).

While I would not classify this as a risk, options holders should be aware that they are not entitled to receive any dividends paid by the underlying company while they hold the options. However, the payment of dividends can cause a small drop in a company's share price after the dividend payment record date passes. This price drop may have a slight effect on the options prices.

Lastly, options trading volumes can be much lower than they are for stocks. This means that the difference, or "spread" between the bid and ask on options that are not traded too frequently, can hit $0.50 or more. This puts you in a relatively difficult position if you want to get out of an options position with maximum profit or minimal loss. The spread between the bid and ask is going to, at best, lead to a smaller profit on the trade, or in the worst-case scenario, a bigger loss. For this reason, veteran options traders usually stick with stocks and indexes that have good liquidity (e.g., AAPL, AMD, TSLA and, SPY).

In summary, options are a valuable tool that an active trader should be familiar with and have the skill to employ as needed. In the following chapters I will expand upon options in further detail, and then present some real-life illustrations of options trading strategies that you can successfully use in order to profit from this trading vehicle.

CHAPTER SUMMARY

The following is a summary of this chapter where I discussed why you might consider trading options over stocks:

- » A trader may prefer to use an options contract over owning the underlying stock or security for the following reasons: options can provide you leverage, options can be used as a hedge on your existing holdings, and options can help you generate additional revenue on your existing holdings.
- » Leverage allows you to use your capital in a way that gets you a better return. Options can provide a much better rate of return compared to a move on the underlying security. However, this cuts both ways as options trades can hit you with more significant percentage losses if you are not on the right side of the trade.
- » Hedging is the equivalent of taking out an insurance policy on an existing position. You can buy puts or calls to protect gains on existing positions.
- » Revenue generation is also possible using options. You can sell OTM puts or calls on existing positions to collect revenue

Why Trade Options

from that sale. Ideally you hope that the security price does not start trading ITM during your hold period.

» Trading options comes with risks that include an increased potential for higher percentage losses. Options can expire worthless if not managed properly, therefore you can lose all the money you paid for the options.

» Options trading volumes can be lower on some securities resulting in a wide bid-ask spread. A wide spread can result in larger losses if you want to exit a position in a hurry.

» Options holders are not entitled to any dividends paid by the underlying company.

CHAPTER 6

Options and the Greeks

After reading this chapter title you may be asking yourself: What does option trading have to do with the Greeks? Quite simply, the term refers to a set of calculations with Greek names that include delta, gamma, and theta. The values derived from these calculations can help the options trader determine the way options prices will react to a shifting market, and underlying security conditions.

This topic can be a little overwhelming for some, but if you are seriously considering trading options, you need to have a basic understanding of the Greeks and how you might be able to use them to your benefit.

There are three that I will discuss in the sections that follow. They each measure a specific factor related to options pricing:

- » Delta
- » Gamma
- » Theta

To simplify things a little for the purposes of this book, I will not discuss the fourth Greek called Vega. The three Greeks I will cover should provide ample information for assessing trading opportunities.

Delta

The delta of an option signals how much the price of that option will change for every $1.00 move (up or down) in the price of the underlying security. For example, let's assume that a Microsoft Corporation (MSFT) call option has a delta of 0.70. That 0.70 tells you that if the MSFT stock price increases by $1.00, the call option will move up by $0.70. Conversely, a drop in MSFT stock of $1.00 with a put option Delta of -0.70 will result in a decrease in the value of the put by about $0.70.

The delta value gives you a sense of how an option price will change as the underlying security price moves up or down. It should be noted that call options will have a positive delta ranging between 0 and 1, while put options will have a negative delta ranging from 0 to -1.

Fortunately, you do not have to be concerned with calculating these numbers. They are published in options tables and are readily available. Be aware that a delta can vary throughout the life of the option as the share price of its underlying asset goes up and down. This is where the gamma enters the equation, which I will explain in the next section.

Options that are close to at-the-money (ATM) usually have a delta value of close to 0.50 (plus for a call, minus for a put). In comparison, options that are in the money (ITM) normally have a delta that is close to a value of + 1 for calls or − 1 for puts. This higher delta reflects the fact that the option will respond more closely to the underlying security move.

Although options that are ITM and ATM are costlier than options that are out of the money (OTM), they do have distinct advantages. For example, a call option that is OTM may only have a delta of 0.30. That means a shift in the price of the underlying security is not going to change the option price as much as it will for an option that is ITM with a delta of 0.70. You can surmise that, in some circumstances there will be greater profit potential in the option that is ITM.

In addition, time decay works against you with an option that is OTM. Every day that passes brings you nearer to the expiry date

Options and the Greeks

of the option. This explains why the delta is lower on options with strikes that are far OTM. Even if there happens to be a move on the price of the underlying security toward the strike price, investors remain skeptical that the security price will get to the strike price, so you do not get as positive a corresponding price move in the option.

Everyone who was involved in the market throughout 2020 has heard stories of traders making large fortunes using options. The delta helps explain how this happens. Let's look at Figure 6.1 which shows a chart of Gamestop Corp. (GME) making a big move higher from a double bottom pattern.

Based on the large price moves GME has made in the past, assume you had decided to take a gamble with money you were willing to lose. With the stock trading at $175.00, you bought a $200.00 call expiring on November 19th (a monthly option). The call would likely have cost you about $2.00 at the time with a delta of 0.25. As the stock started moving higher through dollar increments, the option price initially moved up $0.25 for every $1.00 move.

But as the GME price moved closer to the $200.00 strike price the delta would have also increased. Your call option price is starting to accelerate to the upside, and once GME ripped through the $200 level and then higher, the delta would have been approaching 1.0. This means that every $1.00 in the stock price is matched by a $1.00 increase in the options price, which illustrates how the increasing delta helped you make such large gains.

Obviously, the GME example is an extreme case of how the value of delta can change rapidly with large and swift price changes in the underlying security. The measure of the delta change is called gamma which will be discussed in the following section.

Figure 6.1 Chart of GME showing how the purchase of a $200.00 call option would have turned into a remarkably profitable trade with the help of the delta (chart courtesy of StockCharts.com).

Finally, the delta provides you with an estimated probability as to whether or not the specific option will be ITM at its expiry. For instance, an option with a delta of 0.55 suggests that there is a 55% chance that the option at that particular strike price will close ITM.

In summary, you can glean a lot of worthwhile information from a delta measurement, and that data can be deployed in different ways to help you make successful options trades. Listed below is a summary of important points related to the delta value:

- » Delta value will range from 0 to 1 for calls and 0 to -1 for puts.
- » Options that are far OTM will have delta values closer to 0.
- » Options that are at or well ITM will have delta values closer to 1.
- » As the option's time value decays, the ITM options delta will increase while the OTM options delta will decrease.
- » As volatility increases, the ITM options delta decreases while the OTM options delta increases.

Gamma

The gamma value is another Greek that can be very beneficial when trading options. An option's gamma is a measurement that approximates the rate of change in an option's delta. As mentioned in the previous section, the delta is not a fixed number, and tends to move around depending on various circumstances including shifts in the price of the underlying security and the length of time to the option's expiry.

As the expiration date of an option draws closer, the gamma of ATM options will climb higher. The gamma of the ITM and OTM options will start to decrease, and approach zero, the further the underlying security is trading from the strike price. This happens because options that are significantly in or out of the money, and close to expiry, have little chance of seeing the security price get to the strike price. Barring any short-term radical price moves in the security, these options will either be a solid winner (ITM) or a loser (OTM) for the options buyer.

The implied volatility of a security will also have an impact on the value of gamma. When volatility is low, the gamma of ATM options will be elevated while the gamma for options that are well ITM or OTM will approach zero. When volatility is high, the variation in gamma will tend to be more consistent across all the strike prices. This is caused by the fact that the higher volatility results in a high time value in option prices. Therefore, as the security approaches ITM, the move in the option price will be less dramatic.

I will use Micron Technology, Inc. (MU) as a way to demonstrate the power and effect of gamma. Let's assume MU is trading at $80.00 per share. Concurrently, a monthly $82.00 call option is trading for $2.00 with a delta of 0.4 and a gamma of 0.1. Assume the stock pops up $1.00 to $81.00 per share. The option price should see a corresponding increase to $2.40 ($2.00 plus $0.40 for the delta move). Based on the gamma of 0.1, the delta would be expected to increase from 0.4 to 0.5. The next $1.00 incremental move higher on MU will result in a larger increase in the option value of $0.50.

Based on your position, this attribute can either work in your favor or it can be quite detrimental to your trading account. For example, if your ATM option and its corresponding expiry is rapidly drawing near, a higher gamma will push the option price in your direction if the security price is moving in your favor. Conversely, if your trade is not heading in the direction you had expected, the option price will migrate away from you at a swift pace.

In summary, the gamma measurement informs you of the directional risk of your position. Here are some factors to keep in mind regarding gamma:

» Options with the highest gamma are the most responsive to changes in the price of the underlying security.

» Gamma will be smallest for options that are a long way OTM or ITM.

» Gamma will be highest when the option is near or ATM.

Before moving on to discuss theta, I want to mention that later in the book I will discuss a specific phenomenon that can happen, referred to as a gamma squeeze. These squeezes can result in big share price moves, offering you an opportunity for outsized gains once you have identified them. More about that later.

Theta

The final Greek that I will discuss is the theta. This calculated value represents the time decay of the options. As you are now aware, an option is a contract with an expiry date. For every day that you are holding an options position, it is going to lose a little bit of value if the underlying security price remains the same. The theta quantifies how much value is going to come out of an option each day as it approaches its expiry.

As an example of theta and its impact, consider a put option that you purchased for $5.00 with a current theta of - 0.1. This would imply

Options and the Greeks

that, if there were no significant changes in the underlying security, the value of that option would drop by $0.10 per day. Therefore, after 3 days pass the value of your option would be $4.70. Of course, assuming there are no changes in the security during this 3-day period is not realistic. However, the time value erosion is happening while other factors such as security price and volatility are continuing to influence the option price as well.

It is important to note that the time decay in the value of an option is not linear, and the theta value for an option will change on a daily basis. The graph in Figure 6.2 shows that the closer an option gets to its expiration date, the more the value of that option begins to accelerate to the downside. When there are 60 days to expiry, the day-to-day time decay has a minimal effect on the price of the option. However, take a look at what happens during the last 14 days before expiry. The value curve commences to drop off at a considerably brisker pace, as the time decay has a greater and greater impact on the option price.

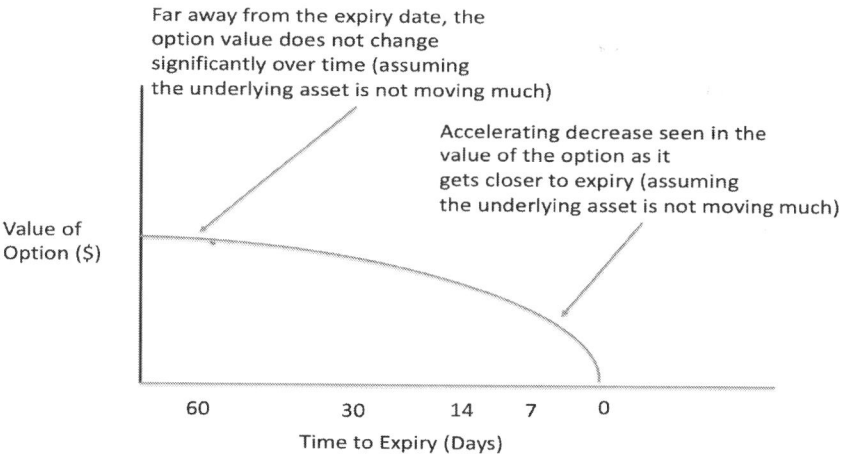

Figure 6.2 - Chart showing how the value of an option accelerates downward the closer it gets to the expiry date.

The accelerated decay can be of benefit or determent depending on your option position. If you are long an option that is OTM, it could have negative repercussions since the value of the option will start to decline faster. However, if you are a seller of an option that is OTM, then the increasing time decay works in your favor as you watch its value plummet. The slide in value offers you an opportunity to buy the option back at a lower price, or to let it expire worthless, keeping the money collected on that option sale.

The theta is usually highest with calls and puts that are ATM, and it will begin to decrease the more ITM or OTM you are. This is one reason why seasoned option traders like to purchase and hold options that are ITM. The further ITM that you are, the less influence the time decay factor will have on an option's value.

One question that comes to mind given the time decay is: Why not buy options with dates more into the future so that the time decay is not so consequential? The answer is quite simply because of the gamma. The gamma tells you how quickly the option price will move in conjunction with changes in the underlying security price. As the gamma decreases with longer expiry dates, any shifting in the price of the underlying security will have a lessened impact on the option price – and that is not likely what an option trader wants to see. The net result of acquiring longer dated options is that the time decay is initially reduced. But, if you go out too far in time, the option will not react sufficiently to changes in the price of the underlying stock.

Here are some points to keep in mind regarding theta:

- » Options with a longer time to expiry will have a theta of close to 0.
- » Theta starts to increase the closer the option gets to the expiry date due to the accelerated time decay.
- » ATM options will tend to have a higher theta compared to ITM or OTM options.
- » Stocks with a higher volatility will have a higher theta.

Greeks Takeaway

In summary, you do not need to master everything there is to know about an option's delta, gamma, and theta. However, having a general understanding of what these Greeks represent will boost your confidence when placing options trades. You will also be able to better adapt and execute strategies that utilize the Greeks.

In the next chapter, I will discuss some specific strategies that you can employ to assist you in making profitable options trades.

CHAPTER SUMMARY

In this chapter we covered the Greeks which are a set of calculations referred to as delta, gamma, and theta. Important points in the chapter include the following:

- » The Greek calculations result in values that can help the options trader determine the way options prices will react to a shifting market and underlying security conditions.
- » The delta value of an option signals how much the price of that option will change for every $1.00 move (up or down) in the price of the underlying security. Delta value will range from 0 to 1 for calls and 0 to -1 for puts.
  - ▷ Options that are far OTM will have delta values closer to 0
  - ▷ Options that are at or well ITM will have delta values closer to 1
  - ▷ As the option's time value decays, the ITM options delta will increase while the OTM options delta will decrease
- » Gamma is a measurement that approximates the rate of change in an option's delta. With an option that has a delta of 0.4 and a gamma of 0.1, an option trader would expect a $0.40 move on the option for the first $1.00 move and then a $0.50 move on the next $1.00 move.

- Options with the highest gamma are most responsive to changes in the price of the underlying security.
  - Gamma will be smallest for options that are a long way OTM or ITM
  - Gamma will be highest when the option is near or ATM
- Theta is the value that represents the time decay of the options. As an option gets closer to its' expiry date, the rate of value decay will increase.
- A theta of - 0.1 would imply, if there were no changes in the underlying security, the value of the associated option would drop by $0.10 per day.
  - Options with a longer time to expiry (30 days or more) will have a theta of close to 0
  - Theta starts to increase the closer the option gets to the expiry date due to the accelerated time decay
  - ATM options will tend to have a higher theta compared to ITM or OTM options

CHAPTER 7
The Gamma Squeeze

As you may already know, there are many different factors that affect the movement in the price of an option. One of those very powerful factors is the option gamma squeeze. In this chapter we will examine the following topics:

- » What is a gamma squeeze
- » Triggers for a gamma squeeze
- » Effect of the gamma squeeze
- » Strategies for managing and trading gamma squeezes

What is a Gamma Squeeze

From the previous chapter we know that gamma represents the rate at which the delta changes (recall delta is a measure of how much an option price will change based on the change of the underlying security).

Another way to think of this is to consider gamma as a measure of the volatility of an option's delta. When an underlying stock price surges higher, it can lead to a corresponding surge in the option gamma. When an option gamma increases, its delta becomes much more sensitive to price movements in the underlying security. The net effect is that movements in the price of the security have an increased impact on the price of the related options.

The gamma squeeze starts when there is a substantial and rapid move in the price of the underlying security. This outsized move can start a chain reaction in the options market due to the fast change in delta, and therefore an increasing gamma. As the underlying stock price approaches and/or crosses important levels, market participants are forced to adjust their option positions quickly which can add to buying or selling activity.

Much of the options selling is done by so called market makers and institutions. For example, when one of these options sellers makes a call option sale, they often hedge (cover) their position by buying the underlying security so they are not exposed to unlimited upside risk. Owning the underlying shares means they will have shares to deliver to a call buyer if they end up ITM on the call. The net effect is that the call seller can be adding to the current buying frenzy which often causes the stock price to get driven higher.

The important levels mentioned earlier are often near option strike prices with a high level of interest. When an option is trading ATM or very close to that level, gamma is typically at its highest point. Therefore, as a stock price moves close to the strike price of an option, the gamma moves up rapidly as well, potentially creating this price squeeze.

Triggers for a Gamma Squeeze

Gamma squeezes can be triggered by any event that causes a stock price to move in a rapid direction, either up or down. These trigger events include the following:

» A technical event such as a breakdown or breakout of a key level of support or resistance respectively. Sometimes a breakthrough of a critical level will trigger a large number of market players to trade the stock, which can generate rapid price movements and increasing gamma.

- » Some fundamental news about a specific company, a sector, or the whole market. It could be positive news like a pharmaceutical company getting a very positive result on a drug trial, or it could be bad news such as a SEC investigation into a company's management practices. Either way, large movements in a stock or index price can cause a corresponding increase in gamma.
- » Occasionally, abnormally large options positions around a specific strike price can cause price movements of the stock to be exaggerated and therefore generate gamma squeezes.
- » Last but not least is the Reddit effect. One of the best illustrations of a gamma squeeze was seen with the trading in GameStop Corp (GME). What started out as a short squeeze coordinated by a small army of online investors, turned into a gamma squeeze as call buying fueled more GME stock buying to hedge those call positions that were sold.

Obviously, for a gamma squeeze to happen a stock must be optionable. It also helps to have an options market for that stock that is fairly actively traded so there is lots of liquidity with a small spread between the bid and the ask.

Effect of the Gamma Squeeze

Gamma squeezes can have a significant impact on your portfolio and if you recognize them happening, they can represent a real opportunity to make some financial gains. The increased volatility will lead to abnormal price movements in both the options and stock price. This will allow an active and alert trader to take advantage of the continued buying or selling driven by a gamma squeeze.

You should be aware that these rapid price movements caused by gamma squeezes can result in sharp and difficult to predict price moves.

Strategies for Managing and Trading Gamma Squeezes

The following are some strategies you can use to take advantage of gamma squeezes when you recognize that they are occurring. These strategies fall in line with any trades that you take, and contain all the elements of managing your risk for the return you expect to receive. They are as follows:

- » Always have a trade plan before you enter any trade. This means know where you will enter, where you will stop out, where you will take profits (could be incremental levels), and know how much you will lose if you are wrong. Your potential loss should not exceed a level you are comfortable with, and not represent a significant percent of your portfolio.

- » Consider using vertical option spreads to reduce your risk in the trade. We will discuss vertical spreads later in this book. This strategy can be employed to reduce the risk of your trade however, it will also limit gains.

- » Avoid going "all-in" on any trade. While you will hear stories of successful you-only-live-once (YOLO) trades, these are basically lottery trades. Some win but most lose. You want to live to trade another day so keep your trades diversified.

Conclusions

Gamma squeezes can be a very powerful force in the options market. These squeezes can offer opportunities for you to take advantage of when they occur. Therefore, it is important for you to understand and recognize when these squeezes are occurring.

When you recognize a gamma squeeze, you need to have the same discipline that you would use in any trade by having a trading plan and sticking with it. Gamma squeezes create outsized price moves and this means you can see outsized gains if you execute your trades correctly.

CHAPTER SUMMARY

In this chapter we discussed the gamma squeeze which can be summarized in the following points:

» One of the most powerful factors that can cause a large price movement in a security is the option gamma squeeze.

» Recall gamma represents the rate at which the delta changes (delta is a measure of how much an option price will change based on the change of the underlying security).

» The gamma squeeze starts when there is a substantial and rapid move in the price of the underlying security. The outsized move can start a chain reaction in the options market due to the fast change in delta and an associated increase in gamma.

» As a stock price moves close to the strike price of an option, the gamma moves up rapidly as well, potentially creating this price squeeze.

» Gamma squeezes can be caused by a fundamental or technical event (for example an earnings release or breakout from a key level of resistance).

» Gamma squeezes can also happen around a strike price where there is a lot of open interest (a large number of existing option contracts).

» Momentum traders and traders jumping into a trade on mass (so called swarm investing) can also cause a gamma squeeze.

» These squeezes cause increased volatility and will lead to abnormal price movements in both the options and stock price.

» To trade and profit from gamma squeezes always have a trading plan, consider the spread between the bid and ask before entering a trade, and manage your risk by avoiding going "all-in". Only risk capital you feel that you can afford to lose.

CHAPTER 8
Options Expiry Dates

When trading options you will have a number of decisions to make. Those decisions will depend a lot on what strategy or strategies you want to employ, and what type of trading you are comfortable with.

For example, many day traders will use options to take advantage of intraday moves, such as a breakout on some good news on a particular security. Other traders are more inclined to use options to swing trade. In this case they may hold the option for a few days to a week or more. Some investors are more interested in holding options for the long-term, expecting a slow and steady move in an underlying security.

In this chapter we will examine your choices for the expiry of an option, and why you might prefer one duration of options over another. We will look at the following option types:

» Daily options

» Weekly options

» Long-term options (LEAPS)

Daily Options

Options with daily expiry dates are available for indexes such as the QQQ, SPY, and IWM. These options primarily exist for day traders looking to take advantage of very short-term trends or moves that happen throughout the trading day.

Daily options can be used to make directional bets on the indexes or non-directional bets. If you think an index is ready to reverse from a downtrend and go back up, you can buy a call. You could also sell a put if you think the security is done going down but not sure if it will make a big move back up.

One positive aspect of trading daily options is that they are very liquid. Therefore, the spread between the bid and ask is small, and it is easy to get out of a position that is not working in your favor. The other advantage in using these short duration options is that you can trade an index at a very low cost compared to taking a trade on an index. For example, 1 SPY call (100 shares) close to the money might cost you $150, while 100 shares of the SPY will cost $43,000 at today's current price.

Many traders will specialize in trading only daily options. They will target areas of prior support or resistance to take positions. They will also look for price action signs such as a reversal doji candle on large volume, or double bottoms to name just a few. For those unfamiliar with those patterns, I strongly suggest additional reading on technical analysis which can be found in many references including my previous books.

Day trading daily options can be profitable for those with an ability to do this type of trading. Anyone attempting to day trade using options should already be very comfortable and knowledgeable in reading the market price action and managing risk. Also be aware you can buy daily options with several days to expiry, but a trader who does this could be doing a swing trade. I will discuss swing trading in the weeklys section below.

Weekly Options

The weekly options usually expire each Friday. The weekly options are used by a lot of day traders and swing traders. As of the writing of this book, there are 521 stocks and 95 exchange-traded funds (ETF) that have weekly options available to trade. A list of these securities can be found at www.cboe.com/available_weeklys.

When actively trading weekly options, it is important to ensure that the volume of option trading is high, so the difference between the bid and ask is not far apart. If you use a hard stop to manage your risk, or you just want to exit the trade quickly, a small spread will ensure that your order will get filled at a reasonable price.

Many day traders and swing traders will use weekly options because they get the same improved percentage gains by trading an option compared to trading the underlying security. The relatively short duration of weekly options may give you slightly improved odds on predicting a security's price direction and target.

If you get the trade right, there are two things that work in your favor. If you have picked a good price for a target, the potential for a good profit is high as the options go ITM. With short term option trades, the time value really starts to erode (remember theta) within the last 2 weeks. Theta can work in your favor if you have sold an option that looks less and less likely to go ITM.

As with most options trades, your trading strategies will determine which strike price you will choose when entering a trade. We will discuss some of these strategies as well as picking price levels later in the book. These are often based on technical and possibly some fundamental analyses.

Long-term Options

If you are more inclined to be a long-term investor, or you just have a good thesis on how a security is going to move well into the future, then you can take a position in Long-term Equity Anticipation Securities. Commonly known as LEAPS, these are options contracts that have a year or more to expiry.

You can use these types of options if you are wanting to trade what you expect to be a prolonged trend in a security. They can also be used as a portfolio management strategy to protect gains or generate income which will be discussed later in the book.

Because of the long time to expiration, LEAPS have a lot of time value built into the price, and therefore they have a higher price versus the shorter-term options. Despite the higher price, they are still cheaper than the underlying security.

Trading LEAPS requires a higher-level view of the market and the underlying security, since you are making an assessment of the price move over a much longer period of time. You might want to rely more heavily on the fundamental analysis of a securities future price moves to determine profit potential, while still looking to prior levels of support or resistance for targeting strike prices.

CHAPTER SUMMARY

In this chapter I discussed the different expiry dates that options can have. The points listed below summarize the chapter:

- » Options expiry dates can range from daily expiration, weekly expiration (every Friday), monthly expiration (the third Friday of the month), to long-term which can be more than a year.
- » The main indexes are the only securities that can be traded with daily expiries. Daily options can be used to make directional bets or non-directional bets on these indexes.
- » Weekly options usually expire each Friday. The weekly options are used by a lot of day traders and swing traders to make directional and non-directional bets on the price of securities.
- » The short duration of weekly options might give you improved odds of determining a security's price direction and target by the time they expire.
- » Longer-term investors can use Long-term Equity Anticipation Securities, (LEAPS). These are options contracts that have a year or more to expiry.

» LEAPS have a lot of time value built into the price, and therefore they are higher priced compared to the shorter-term options. Despite the higher price, they are still cheaper than the underlying security.

» LEAPS requires a higher-level view of the market and the underlying security, while the shorter duration options are used by traders for expected short-term moves in price.

CHAPTER 9
Purchasing and Selling Options

Now that you understand how options work and are priced, I will discuss some specific strategies for trading options. There are numerous techniques and strategies that can be employed using options. In this chapter, I will begin by examining two basic and relatively straightforward directional trading strategies. These methods can be categorized as follows:

» Purchasing options - put or call

» Selling options - put or call

Each of these approaches will be explained and illustrated separately below.

Purchasing Options – Put or Call

The most basic options trading strategy is going long on puts or calls. When you go long on a call option, it means you are bullish on the prospects of the underlying security. In other words, you are expecting the price of the security to rise, which should result in an increase in the value of the option. The amount of time that you choose to hold this trade can vary significantly. It may be as brief as several minutes (a day trade), to a few months or even longer.

To make a directional options trade, an investor or trader needs to be active and connected to the markets due to the time-sensitive nature of options. The shorter the period is to expiry, the more in tune you must be. Generally speaking, if you are a "buy and hold" investor, then short-term options trading is probably not right for you.

Similar to trading stocks, an options trade needs to be thought out and planned in advance. Let's begin by looking at the purchase of a call option. The first step in buying a call option is finding a security that is trending up or one that you suspect is ready to move higher. Once a suitable security is identified, you should decide on a strike price and an expiry date for the call option. These decisions will depend on your analysis of the underlying security, including how soon you anticipate it to move and by how much.

Do you recall from chapter 6 the commentary regarding the measure of an option's delta? The delta tells you that a security does not have to get to the strike price - it only needs to start moving in that direction well before the expiry date. The option price will move up when the price of the stock moves up. This gives you the opportunity to profit by selling all or part of your options holdings well before the expiry date.

In chapter 5, I wrote about why you might decide to buy a call option and not the underlying security. For instance, you may sense that Tesla, Inc. (TSLA) is going to trend up during the next several days. You could buy 100 shares of TSLA at its current price of $270.00 per share (for a total payment of $27,000.00), or you could buy 1 ITM $270.00 call expiring at the end of the week for $5.50 per contract. That would cost you $550.00 (remember, 1 call option equals 100 shares) with a delta of 0.50. Now for every $1.00 move higher in TSLA, you will get a $0.50 increase in the price of your option. That $0.50 move is almost a 10% return on your option investment, while the $1.00 increase in the price of TSLA of your TSLA shares equates to a 0.3% return. This trade offers leverage and the possibility of a considerably greater percentage gain on your investment if TSLA moves higher in your favor.

The same methodology applies to buying puts, but in this case, you are banking on the underlying security to fall in price. Do not forget that buying a put is buying a right to sell a security at some strike price prior to the expiry of the option. You are taking a short position on the security without the risk of an unlimited loss. With a put option, the most you can lose is what you paid for the option plus the commission on the trade.

For example, imagine the loss you would have experienced shorting GameStop Corp. (GME) stock in December 2020 at $15.00 per share, and then watching it rise to over $480.00 per share in late January 2021. Conversely, buying put options would have limited your maximum loss to the cost of the put options.

The strike price you chose for your option will be partially dependent on the duration of time that you intend to hold the option. If you are a day trader, then your strike price should be close to or ITM with a higher delta. If you pick a strike price too far away from the current price, the option will be cheaper, but that is because there is a much lower likelihood that the price will get to the strike before the end of the day. The delta is lower for OTM options as well, so the incremental move on the option price will be lower for every unit move on the underlying security.

That is not to say that an OTM option purchase will not work well for a day trade. If it is fairly close to the current price and the security moves aggressively in your favor (maybe even moving to ITM) then, in this scenario, your return could be even better compared to an ITM option purchase.

Let's look at an example trade on Coinbase Global Inc. (COIN) shown in Figure 9.1. The stock had been seeing some strength in prior days and looked ready to take off at the open on July 11, 2023. As a day trader, you could have bought the shares around $81.00 at the open, or alternatively you could have purchased weekly $81.00 call options for $2.50. Assuming you took profits after the big run up to $90.00, you would have made a tidy $9.00 per share gain on the stock trade which equates to an 11% gain on the trade. However, the $81.00 weekly calls, which originally traded for $2.50, would have sold for around $10.50 which is a 320% gain on the money invested. This trade opportunity really illustrates the leverage power that option's hold.

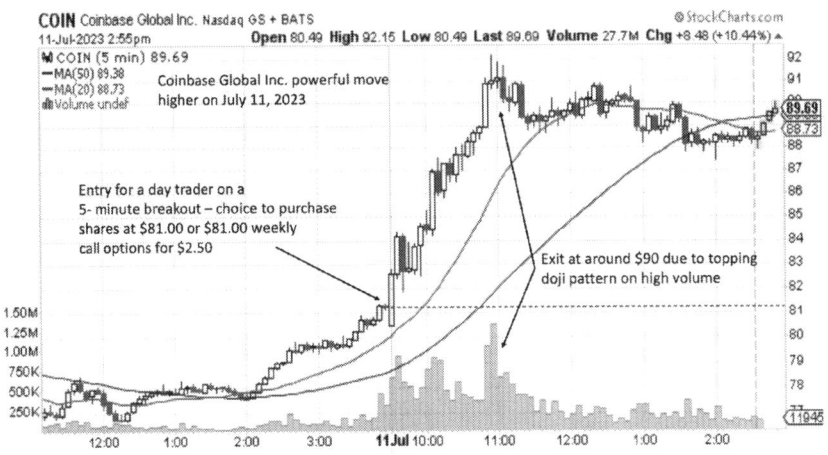

Figure 9.1 Chart showing COIN share price powerful move higher with a choice to buy the stock at $81.00 or the $81.00 weekly call option (chart courtesy of StockCharts.com).

If you are swing trading or taking a long-term position trade, then you may want to consider options that have an OTM strike. The options will be cheaper but compared to a day trade, you have some time on your side for the underlying security to move toward the strike price. This can work in your favor because the delta will increase as the security price gets closer to the strike price. This is where gamma is on your side and the returns on the options can be much better compared to purchasing ITM options to start.

Let's look at a swing trade example shown in Figure 9.2. NVDA was trading at $250.00 on March 16, 2023. You could have purchased a NVDA ITM $250.00 call expiring May 19, 2023 (monthly option) for about $8.00 versus an OTM $270 call for $1.50. On the expiry date of May 19, NVDA finished the trading day at about $312.00. If you had held both options to expiry, the ITM call would have gone from an $8.00 value to $62.00 ($312.00 close price minus $250.00 strike price), which is by any measure an incredible return. However, the OTM option went from a value of $1.50 to $42.00 ($312.00 close price minus $270.00 strike price) which is an even better percentage return on your investment.

Figure 9.2 Chart showing a swing trade on NVDA to compare outcome of a stock purchase versus a call option purchase (chart courtesy of StockCharts.com).

The same directional trades can be executed with put options if you are feeling negative about the price action of a security. The leverage of options still applies to puts which will give you a much better percentage gain. As I discussed above, going short exposes you to almost unlimited risk as a stock can go up in price many times over on some positive news. When you purchase a put option, your risk of loss is limited to the amount you paid for the put.

In summary, trading options as a directional play requires the identical kind of due diligence that goes into buying and selling the underlying security itself. The following are steps to observe when making options trades:

How to Trade Options

- » Scans and Research – whether you are day trading, swing trading or taking a long-term position, you should have a process in place to find trading opportunities.
- » Filter – make sure the options you are trading are relatively liquid. This means the spreads between the bid and ask are small and they are actively traded, so you can exit easily and with minimal slippage (price difference between bid and ask).
- » Profit Targets and Stops – as with any security trade, you must have a trading plan for your options trade. If you do not have one in place you are gambling. You can certainly win when you are gambling, but if you stay in a casino long enough, you will go broke. The market is exactly the same. Having a well-thought-out plan in advance can also help you manage the emotional aspect of trading. Trades do not always unfold as hoped for once you have opened a position. A logical plan can assist you in holding through any short-term dips while you wait for the trade to go in the direction you expect it to in the longer term.
- » Expiry Date – based on your analysis of the security, you need to estimate how many minutes, hours, days, or weeks it will take for a notable move in price. In chapter 6, I referenced that the value of an option will start to drop significantly as its expiration approaches. For traders with a longer-term view, you want to have a future expiry date that is sufficient to catch the shift in price before you get too close to the expiry date. For day traders or swing traders, you will be looking for a relatively big move in the underlying security price over a short period of time.
- » Strike Price – your analysis of the security should also be utilized to determine the strike price. Many options traders buy options with a strike price that is a little ITM with a delta of at least 0.60 (or greater). Others choose options that are close to the price but a little OTM. Although it is a matter of personal choice, your assessment of near-term price moves

should be a part of your decision. If you select a strike price that is markedly OTM, the option price will be much lower, but so will the probability of making a profitable trade ahead of the expiry of the option.

» Monitor the Trade – again, just like any security trade, it is important to actively monitor your position to verify that the trading plan you have developed is being followed (with minimal emotion).

Selling Options – Put or Call

In the preceding section, I discussed buying a call (or a put) as a method to profit from a rising (or falling) underlying security price. As an option purchaser, you are hoping for a move in the direction of your bet. If this does not occur, then you will almost certainly end up with a losing trade.

The other strategy that you can employ that could improve your odds on having a winning trade is to be the seller of the options. However, those improved odds will also limit your upside gains as well as putting your capital at greater risk. Your gains are limited when selling options because the most you can make on the trade is the amount you collected from the buyer when the options expire OTM.

However, recall that a buyer of options can potentially get outsized gains of more than 100% with a well-placed trade so as a seller, you could lose much more than you collect in premium (the amount you collect on an options sale is often referred to as the "premium").

As the seller of options, you are essentially becoming a banker. The option buyer pays you money for entering into the option contract, and in return you take on the liability of having to fulfil that contract at a future date. Of course, you may choose to trade the contract to someone else before the expiry date, which gives you a way to manage your risk by freeing yourself of that liability.

It can be a bit of a confusing concept, so think of it in opposites. If you think a security price is going up, you buy a call. If you do the opposite and sell the call option, then you are making a bearish bet on the security and expecting the price to drop. The positive aspect of selling options is that it is also possible to have a profitable trade even if the security moves very little after you sell the option. This is due to the time value that is baked into the value of the option. Recall theta and how the value of the option decays as the expiry date draws closer.

Let's consider a scenario where you believe a security has stopped dropping in price. You could buy a call option or you could decide to sell a put instead. By selling that put you are betting that a security has, at the very least, stopped dropping in price or is ready to reverse and go higher. Remember that buying a put is a bearish trade so doing the opposite and selling a put is taking a bullish position.

Let's look at an example in Figure 9.3 where Tesla Inc. (TSLA) had a big run up in price through May and June 2023 on news Elon Musk had turned the day-to-day oversight of Twitter over to someone else. Investors believed that this would allow him to get his focus back on the car company.

The big run eventually got exhausted as illustrated by a double top that occurred around July 3, 2023 at a price of $280.00. Seeing this topping action was an opportunity to sell $300.00 weekly calls for about $150 per contract ($1.50 x 100 shares per contract).

The $300.00 strike was a good level because it was still OTM, and therefore gave the option seller a little room to be wrong on the timing if TSLA popped a little higher before reversing. Don't forget, with any trade you must have an exit plan if things do not work as expected, so a break back above $280.00 on TSLA would have been your stop out on the trade.

Selling $300.00 calls was a good strategy because TSLA stock is a favorite with retail investors, and a significant drop in price was not likely in the cards, therefore buying puts may not have paid off.

However, from the put sale perspective, option premiums were high so you collected a good amount of money per contract.

Now TSLA just needed to stop going up, which it did. As the week came to an end, the option contract value eroded away with theta. You then have the choice of buying back some or all of the puts at a much lower price or you could just let them expire worthless at the end of the week. You keep the money paid to you by the contract buyer.

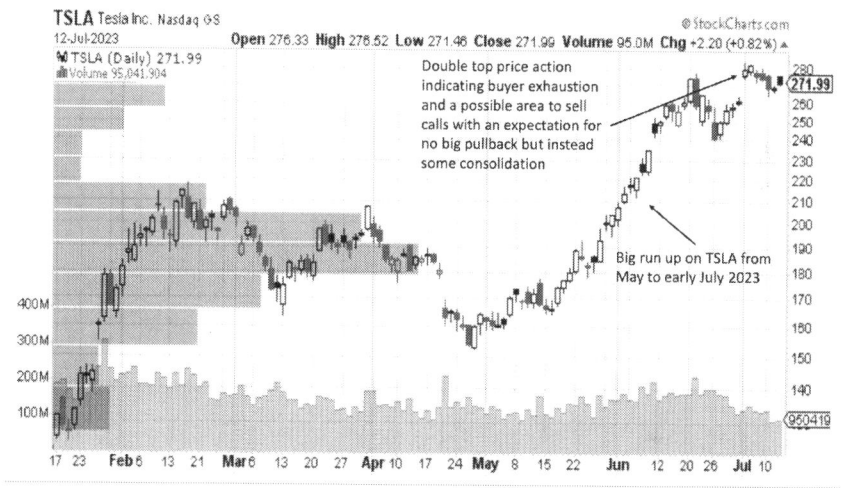

Figure 9.3 Chart of TSLA illustrating a good setup for selling call options (chart courtesy of StockCharts.com).

It is worth emphasizing that selling calls and puts without any protection can be very risky, especially when swing trading. Holding positions overnight when the markets are closed exposes you to the potential of unexpected news events that can negatively affect your position. Imagine if some news came out regarding TSLA that caused the stock to move above $300.00 at the open of the next trading day. The cost to buy back your $300.00 call options would be many times in excess of the $150.00 premium you might have collected for selling them.

Employing this strategy as a day trade is much less risky because, if an option price moves against you, you can exit immediately and limit your loss. With swing trades there are ways to protect yourself from a large loss using vertical spreads, which I will discuss in the following chapter. Another way to limit your risk is to keep your position small so your potential loss is not a devastating one.

CHAPTER SUMMARY

In this chapter, I discussed the process of buying and selling options to make straight-forward directional trades on securities. The salient points of the chapter are summarized below:

- » The most basic options trading strategy is to buy (go long) a put or call.
- » Going long a put or call is essentially making a bet on the future direction of an underlying security within a defined period of time. When you buy a call, you are expecting the price of the underlying security to go higher. When you buy a put you are hoping the security will move lower in price.
- » Just like trading a stock, you need to plan your options trades by picking logical strike prices, expiry dates, and the points at which you will either take profits or stop out. The type of trading you are doing will impact these decisions depending on whether you are day trading, swing trading, or taking a long-term view.
- » Day traders will be more inclined to take short-term expiry dates and close to or ITM options.
- » Swing traders and position traders can look at options that are more OTM because time is on their side.
- » The second simple directional options trade strategy is to be the seller of the options. The seller takes the opposite view compared to the options buyer. For example, a call option buyer

thinks the security will go up whereas the call seller believes the security price will either go down, or at the very least, move very little so the value of the option decays.

» The put seller is taking the view that the underlying security price is done going down and will either hold where it is or reverse and start going higher. They are essentially making a bullish bet.

» The advantage of selling options is that you can benefit from the security going the direction you hope or not moving much in price at all.

» The disadvantage is that you have limited your gain to the amount you collected as a premium during the sale of the options, compared to buying options which can give you more than 100% gains if the trade really works well.

» The other big disadvantage of selling options is that it exposes you to a significant loss of many times what you collected in premium. In comparison, the most you can lose buying options is the amount you spent on the position.

CHAPTER 10

Vertical Spreads

In the previous chapter, I discussed the most basic options strategy that can be used to make a directional bet on the price of a security. In this chapter we will examine how you can lower the cost of making that directional bet. This strategy is referred to as a vertical spread, with two potential trade setups that can be categorized as follows:

» Buying vertical spreads – put or call
» Selling vertical spreads – put or call

Each of these approaches will be explained and illustrated separately below.

Buying Vertical Spreads – Put or Call

Once you have a solid understanding of buying or selling puts and calls, your next step is to study the vertical spread strategy. Adding this strategy to your trading tool box will expand your ability to execute successful options trades by lowering the cost of your trades while also reducing risk.

There are 2 vertical spreads that I will explain in this section of the chapter: the "bull call spread" and the "bear put spread". As the names imply, the first is used when you expect a security price will go up, and the second is used when you expect a drop in price.

Establishing a bull call spread involves purchasing a call that is usually ITM or close to ITM, and then selling a call that is at a higher strike price OTM. It is important to mention that both calls must have the same expiration date.

For instance, Microsoft Corporation (MSFT) was trading at $245.00 per share in the middle of February 2021. If you believed MSFT was going to increase further through the rest of the month and into March, rather than purchasing the shares outright, you could have bought an ATM $245.00 call option expiring March 19th for approximately $7.00 per contract (recall a contract is 100 shares equating to a cost of $700.00). That meant MSFT would have had to climb to at least a level of $252.00 to be profitable (the strike price of $245.00 plus the $7.00 per contract cost of the call). That is not necessarily a huge shift in its price, but MSFT still had a way to go before the trade would become profitable.

This is where you could have utilized a vertical call spread to lower that break even cost. In this situation, you would collect some money from selling a higher strike price call. If you decided that while MSFT would increase in price, it would not go to as high as $255.00 per share, you could have sold a $255.00 strike price call, collecting $3.00 per contract for that sale. Now MSFT only has to rise by $4.00 per share (to $249.00 per share) for your trade to be profitable with this bull call spread (the cost of purchasing the $245.00 call at $7.00 per contract minus the money brought in from selling the $255.00 call at $3.00 per contract). The Table 10.1 below illustrates how the call spread reduces the break-even price.

	Option purchase	Option sale	Net option cost
Strike price of call option used	$245.00	$255.00	
Call option price	Buy for +$7.00	Sell for -$3.00	$4.00
Break-even price	$252.00		$245.00+$4.00=$249.00

Table 10.1 A table illustrating how a call spread lowers the break-even cost on an option trade.

Vertical Spreads

For those that prefer to see how the trade might work in a graph form, you can refer to Figure 10.1. This shows how profits on the trade will move as the MSFT share price reaches the break-even price of $249.00 per share, and tops out at the $255.00 level, assuming they are held to expiration.

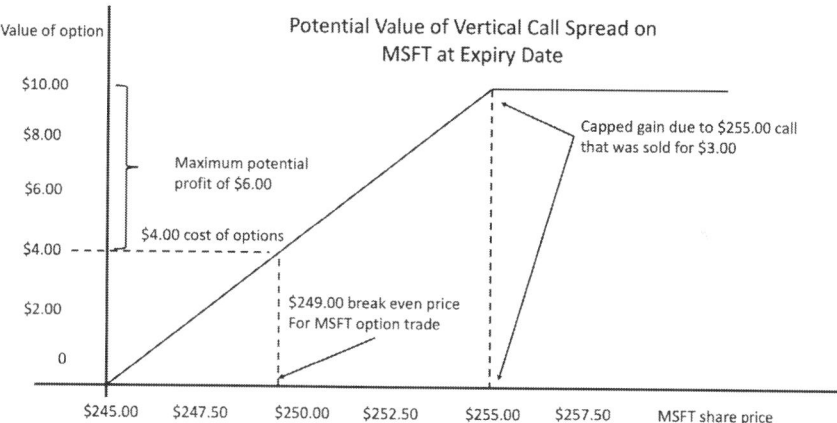

Figure 10.1 Graph showing value of call option spread as the share price of MSFT moves higher. Profits are capped at the $255.00 level.

As you can see from the graph, the downside of a vertical spread strategy is that you are capping the profit that you can make on the trade. In this example, if MSFT had traded over $255.00 prior to the expiry date, then the sale of the $255.00 call would have become a losing position on that part of the trade. That would be okay, because the loss you suffered on the sale of the call was more than balanced by the gain you would receive from the $245.00 call that you were long. Therefore, the most that you can profit on this trade is $6.00 per contract, which is the difference between your break-even price of $249.00 and the upside cap of $255.00.

From a positive perspective, MSFT only needed to trade above $249.00 for the bull call spread to be profitable. As an aside, always remember that selling calls is considerably riskier if you do not have cover. In this case, your cover was the $245.00 call. If taken to expiry, and MSFT was at $260.00 on that day, you would have been obligated to sell MSFT to another party for $255.00 per share (losing $5.00 per share on that part of the trade). Nevertheless, you also had a contract with a different party that required them to sell you an equal number of shares at $245.00 per share (a gain of $15.00 per contract). Therefore, you were covered and your risk was eliminated on any significant upward price move.

Alternatively, the bear put spread can be used when you suspect a security's price is going to trade lower in the coming days, weeks, or months. To utilize this strategy, you would buy one put and then sell a second put at a lower strike price. As with the bull call spread, both puts must have the same expiry date.

Continuing with MSFT, let's assume that you thought the stock was about to fall. You accordingly bought an ATM put at a $245.00 strike price for a cost of $7.00 per contract. Now in order for this trade to be profitable by the expiry of the put, MSFT would have to drop below $238.00 ($245.00 less the $7.00 per contract put cost).

To complete the bear put spread, you would sell a $230.00 put with the same expiry date (and let's say you collected $2.50 per contract from the contract buyer). The $2.50 per contract, earned from the option sale, can be used to partially offset the $7.00 per contract cost of the put you had purchased.

Now for the MSFT bear put spread trade to be profitable, the stock price needs to drop to $240.50 (the cost of purchasing the $245.00 put at $7.00 per contract less the money brought in selling the $230.00 put at $2.50 per contract). Table 10.2 below illustrates how the put spread reduces the break-even price.

Vertical Spreads

	Option purchase	Option sale	Net option cost
Strike price of put	$245.00	$230.00	
Put option price	Buy for +$7.00	Sell for -$2.50	$4.50
Break-even price	$238.00		$245.00-$4.50=$240.50

Table 10.2 A table illustrating how a put spread lowers the break-even cost on an option trade.

Do not forget that the sale of the $230.00 put was covered by the purchase of the $245.00 put. Therefore, you are not exposed to a loss if the MSFT price drops under the $230.00 per share level. However, this also curbs your profits because an MSFT price below $230.00 means you would start losing money on that component of the trade. You would still be profitable on the overall trade since you were holding the $245.00 put (which was significantly ITM).

Again, for those that prefer to see how the trade might work in graph form, you can refer to Figure 10.2 which shows how profits on the trade will move as the MSFT share price reaches the break-even price of $240.50 per share, and tops out at the $230.00 level assuming they are held to expiration.

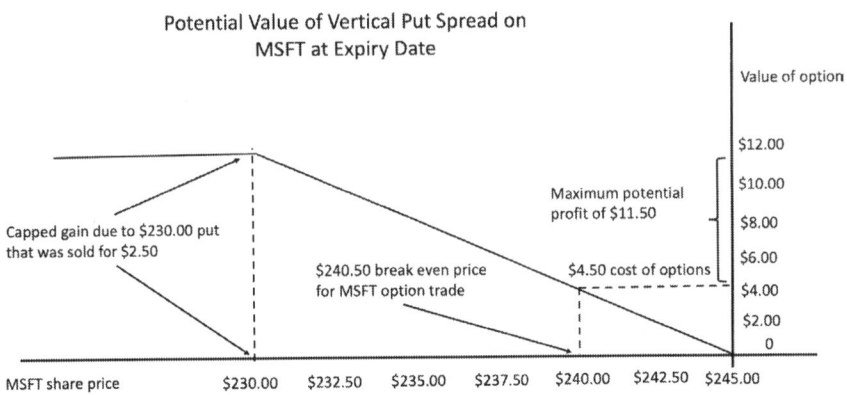

Figure 10.2 Graph showing value of put option spread as the share price of MSFT moves lower. Profits are capped at the $230.00 level.

The question that remains is, "When would you use a vertical spread rather than make a straight-forward purchase of a call or put?" You will find that there are times when you will want to be aggressive with your options trades, and there will be other occasions when you may want to be more risk adverse.

If you are feeling very confident in the direction the security is going, and you expect the move to be more extreme in nature, then you will not want to restrict the profit potential of the trade by creating a vertical spread. If you are feeling less confident, or just want to be conservative with your options trades, you can utilize a vertical spread. In picking levels to buy and sell calls or puts, you can refer to your charts, as they will assist you in locating prior areas of resistance and support to target with your strike prices.

Let's examine how you could have used a bull call spread with MSFT in January 2021. In the chart of MSFT in Figure 10.3, you can see that this stock had been experiencing resistance around the $225.00 level at several points in the past. Once you have conducted sufficient technical analysis, you will come to realize that when an important resistance level is broken to the upside, a security is likely to keep moving higher. Upon noticing this MSFT breakout, you may

Vertical Spreads

have chosen to make a bullish trade on MSFT by employing a bull call spread.

In this instance, you could have bought a $230.00 weekly call on Monday, January 25th for, say, $4.50 per contract. You may have then selected Friday, February 5th to be the expiry date for the call so as to give some time for the stock to move higher. To reduce the cost of the trade and to improve your chances of making a profit, you might also have sold an OTM call (with the same expiry date) at $240.00 for $1.50 per contract. Generally speaking, you should go up at least 2 strike price levels when selling the upside options. With this MSFT bull call spread trade, you would have been in a profitable position if, before its expiry, the stock price had risen above $233.00 ($230.00 plus $3.00 per contract which is the net cost of the 2 calls).

Figure 10.3 - MSFT chart demonstrating how levels of prior resistance create a level of future support for a bull call spread option play (chart courtesy of StockCharts.com).

As Figure 10.3 clearly shows, your trade would have been quite profitable with MSFT moving up and through the $240.00 price level. Unfortunately, the call you sold at $240.00 capped your profit (hindsight is always 20/20) but you would have made a tidy profit of $7.00 per contract on the $230.00 call that you had purchased.

The chart of Square Inc. (SQ) in Figure 10.4 details one additional example of a bull call spread. You will note that from December 2020 and into January 2021 there were clear areas of support at $200.00 and clear areas of resistance at $240.00. In the final week of January 2021, volume began to increase and then, on January 27th, the price of SQ traded down to the $200.00 level, forming an indecision doji candle on the daily chart. Believing that SQ had yet again probably found support, I concluded it was a good setup for a bull call spread. (As you can see on the chart, SQ subsequently did bounce in price.)

You could have put on a bull call spread with a date to expiry of 23 days (February 19th), by purchasing a $200.00 ITM call for a cost of about $20.00 per contract. To complete the spread strategy, you could have sold a $240.00 call with the same expiry date and collected $8.00 per contract from the call buyer. The sale of the $240.00 call would have reduced the cost of this trade to $12.00 per contract (remember, one call contract represents 100 shares, so the total cost was $1,200.00).

As it turned out, although SQ blasted above that $240.00 level, the whole trade was still very profitable due to the $200.00 call that was purchased. The price gain was capped because of the $240.00 call sale. The overall options trade cost $12.00 per contract, leaving a net gain of $28.00 per contract ($40 per contract gain between the $200.00 and $240 call less the net cost of the option of $12.00 per contract).

Many traders who deploy vertical spreads will choose an expiry date 20 to 40 days into the future. You do not have to faithfully obey this rule, but the further away an expiry date is, the more time there will be for the anticipated price move to occur. You will recall from chapter 6 that the value of an option will start to accelerate down as its expiry date approaches.

Vertical Spreads

Figure 10.4 - Chart of SQ showing how you could have used a bull call spread to profit from a bounce off of historical support of $200.00 (chart courtesy of StockCharts.com).

In summary, setting up vertical spreads requires diligence similar to the directional bet trades I discussed in the previous section. I will not repeat the criteria they have in common, however there are some specific criteria to consider when using vertical spreads:

» With regard to strike prices, you should buy an option with a strike price that is very close to, or a little ITM. You should subsequently pick a second option that is in an area OTM where the underlying security will find resistance for a call option or support for selling a put option. Generally speaking, go to at least the second-strike price OTM.

» When selling the OTM option, look to collect a minimum of 30% of the spread between the 2 options. In other words, if you are buying a call at $100.00 and selling a call at $110.00, you should ensure you bring in no less than $3.00 per contract on the sale of the call (30% of the $10.00 difference).

81

» You must carefully monitor the trade. Do not permit your losses to grow by more than 50% of your initial investment.

» Once you are at a 50% profit position, you ought to assess whether it is prudent to exit some, or possibly all of the position.

Vertical spreads offer an opportunity to make a directional bet on the price move of a security at a lower cost, but you need to be aware that lowering the cost of the trade also limits your potential profits on the trade.

Selling Vertical Spreads – Puts and Calls

Now let's look at selling vertical spreads. The reason for using this trade strategy is not the same as we discussed in the previous section, which is to lower the price point where you are making a profit. In this case, you want to make a directional bet on the price of a security, but you want to limit your potential loss if the trade does not work out as hoped.

In chapter 9 I discussed how you can sell puts or calls to collect a premium from the buyer. Similarly, this trade strategy involves selling an ITM or near ITM option and collecting that premium. Then you would simultaneously purchase an OTM option at a strike price that is higher in the case of a call or lower in the case of a put. You now have a trade position in place that will limit your loss in case of an unforeseen negative event.

Let's look at an example where you could sell a vertical spread on Meta Platforms Inc. (META) based on the chart shown in Figure 10.5. META has been trading in a range over the past couple of weeks, and looks ready to break out higher. However, you are not that confident about the break out, and you think it may just continue to churn sideways in the range shown on the chart. One possible trade in this situation is to sell a lower priced $277.50 weekly put. If it continues to trade in a narrow range, at the end of the week you keep the premium collected on the option sale. If it does break out higher, you still get to keep the premium because the put becomes less and less valuable.

Vertical Spreads

If you are a more conservative trader and do not want to take the risk of selling a naked put, you can buy a put option that is further down and OTM such as a $270.00 put. You have now defined your risk and if some bad news comes out regarding META, and the stock drops, the $270.00 put will gain in value as you lose money on the $277.50 put you sold.

Figure 10.5 Chart showing a setup to sell a downside put to collect premium with protection at a lower price by purchasing a $270.00 put (chart courtesy of StockCharts.com).

The pricing cost on this trade would have worked as follows. Selling the $277.50 weekly put would have allowed you to collect $3.50 per contract. Buying a $270.00 put would have cost you $0.80 per contract. After collecting the money from selling the one put and buying the other, you would be up $2.70 per contract ($270.00 on the 100-share contract). Now, if META churns sideways or goes higher, you keep the $270.00 at expiry, or close some or all of the trade earlier for less profit.

On the flip side, if there is some really bad news that comes out and META drops significantly to $270.00 or below, your worst possible outcome is a loss of $480.00 per contract (loss of $750.00 on put sale at $277.50 but adding back the $270.00 collected for the put sale).

Purchasing the OTM $270.00 put saved you from a much worse loss if the price had dropped even further below that level.

You can apply the same principal to selling upside calls if you think a security is going to churn sideways or trend lower. Selling one call and then purchasing a call at a higher strike allows you to limit your upside risk if the trade does not work in your favor.

While I covered selling vertical spreads in this chapter, it is not a strategy that is as commonly used compared to purchasing a vertical spread. But as I discussed, it does provide you with a way of limiting your risk on a short option trade.

CHAPTER SUMMARY

In this chapter, I discussed the process of buying options and selling options simultaneously to make directional trades on securities at a lower cost compared to straight-forward option purchases. The strategy called vertical spreads can be summarized as follows:

- » Vertical spreads can either be applied to securities you believe are going higher or lower. A bull call spread is done when you believe the price is going higher but could be capped.
- » A bear put spread can be used when you believe the underlying security price is going down, but might find support at a lower level which will limit its downside.
- » A bull call spread is done with the purchase of a call that is close to or ITM, and at the same time, selling another call at a higher strike price (same expiry price). The premium taken in by selling the call offsets some of the purchase cost of the ITM call, and therefore lowers your breakeven price on the trade.
- » A bear put spread is done with the purchase of a put that is close to or ITM, and at the same time, selling another put at a lower strike price (same expiry dates). The premium taken in

Vertical Spreads

by selling the put offsets some of the purchase cost of the ITM put, and therefore lowers your breakeven price on the trade.
- » The obvious advantage of the strategy is that you can be profitable on the trade with less of a move on the price of the underlying security.
- » The disadvantage of this strategy is that it caps your potential gains once the price of the sold option is reached.
- » Another less commonly used trade strategy is to sell an ITM (or close to ITM) option and buy an option that is further OTM. This is referred to as selling a vertical spread, and is similar to the strategy of selling options that I discussed in chapter 9. However, with the vertical spread, you have defined your maximum loss through the purchase of the OTM options.

CHAPTER 11
Covered Calls and Puts

The next option strategy I will highlight is known as a covered call (or put). The reference to "covered" means that you already have the underlying security in your portfolio. Based on this existing portfolio position, you will either sell an OTM call against your long position, or sell an OTM put against the short position you are holding. Recall that selling the option allows you to collect the premium from the buyer.

This strategy is primarily used when you believe that the underlying security is not going to make a big price move one way or the other. Using this covered options approach is a way to leverage your current position, so that you can collect an additional revenue stream at the option expiry date while the stock churns in a narrow range.

Of course, there is a downside in that your existing share position could be taken out of your account, if the underlying security price moves past the strike price at expiry. As an example, let's review Figure 11.1, where I used a covered call strategy on a United States Steel Corporation (X) stock position I held in my account.

On February 2nd, 2021, X announced that they would be undertaking a secondary offering of shares for the purpose of raising capital. The day following their news release I noticed on my charts that a significant sell-off was unfolding. X's secondary offering was done at the $16.00 level, and as expected, the price of X promptly dropped to that level. In these circumstances, I presumed that the pullback would hold at around the offering price.

I liked the fundamental story of X as a Covid-19 recovery trade, and it was obvious that, going forward, the new political administration would be spending a lot of money on infrastructure projects. Further, from a technical perspective, X was holding at $16.00. Accordingly, both the fundamental and technical analyses were telling me that X was a buy. Because I thought X might take a bit of time to rally back, I decided a covered call strategy would be a good way to play this situation. It would allow me to generate income on my holding while I waited.

I purchased the stock at a little over the $16.00 level and then I sold some OTM $18.00 calls against the holding. This $18.00 weekly call provided me in the neighborhood of $20.00 per call in revenue. With a 1,000-share position, I was selling 10 option contracts per week for a total of just under $200.00 after commissions. Collecting $200 per week on my $16,000.00 investment in X generates about 1.25% per week, which is a decent annual return even if the stock price stays around the $16.00 level.

My plan was to keep selling these calls each week, anticipating they would expire worthless every Friday. As one weekly call expired, I would write another, repeating the process, and taking in a premium each week.

This strategy worked well until Friday, March 5th when the stock closed a touch above the strike price at $18.15 per share. Since I felt there was the potential for X to continue higher in price, I chose to get out of that week's obligations to sell the shares by purchasing back the $18.00 calls I had previously sold that week. I did this near the market close, almost immediately before that week's calls expired. This purchase cost me about the same amount that I had collected for selling the calls earlier in the week.

In this case it turned out to be an advantageous decision to hold on to X, as the stock maintained its upward direction in the days to come. The chart of X in Figure 11.1 shows how the price went on to retest the prior high of $24.00 from January 12th. It encountered expected resistance at that level, leading me to sell some of my shares in the vicinity of that price.

Covered Calls and Puts

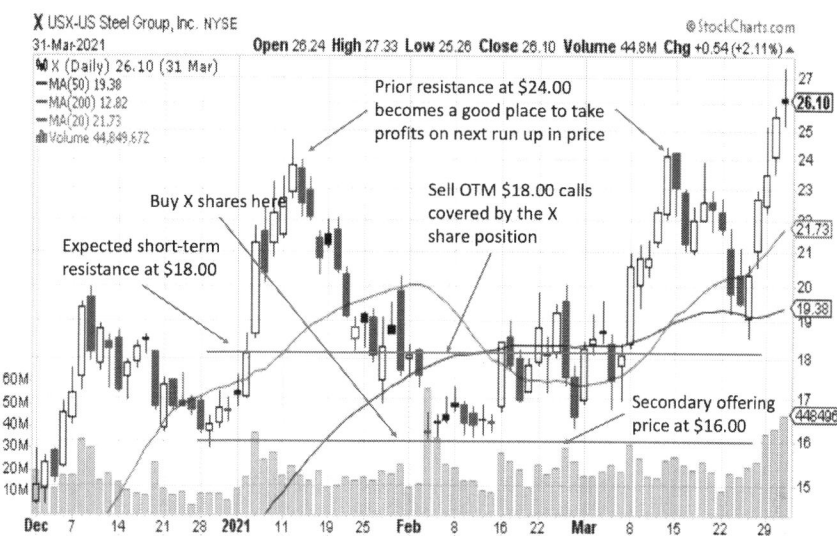

Figure 11.1 - Chart of X illustrating a solid place to enter a position and where to sell calls in order to generate revenue (chart courtesy of StockCharts.com).

When you are selling calls or puts to bring in revenue, you need to be prepared for the day that the option will end up ITM as it did with X. You can then allow the shares to be taken away from you, or alternatively, you can buy back the option. Regardless of your choice, this trade will be profitable. It is a matter of whether you think it is beneficial to extend your hold on the existing underlying position, or if you believe it is better to let it go and move on to the next opportunity.

The other scenario that can occur is when the underlying shares move against you. For instance, if X had started to drop in price, I would begin to lose money on my X shares. But the calls would also dip in value, making them cheaper to buy back. This is where your trading plan is important. Had X slid below my stop out price of $16.00, I would have seriously considered exiting the trade completely. Protecting your capital must be your priority. The loss of a key support level on the underlying security would be apt to result in a much greater loss, even if the calls go to $0.00.

Now, let's look at another example of this strategy that involves selling a covered put when you are holding a short position in a security. On February 3rd, 2023 PayPal Holdings, Inc. (PYPL) showed a strong price reversal pattern. The gravestone doji indicated that investors had turned bearish on the stock and it was likely going to head lower. Seeing this setup for a reversal you could have shorted the shares at just over $85.00

The stock continued to sell off through February and turned into a very profitable trade. You could have covered part of your position on the way down, but you were also eyeing the gap up move in price that the stock made December 31st, 2022. Most technical traders will watch for a stock price to return and "fill that gap" before bouncing back. Referring to Figure 11.2, you can see that is what happened on March 13th.

On the gap fill you had several strategies that you could have implemented. One would have been to cover the remaining PYPL shares that you were short. However, if you felt there was more downside to go on the price, you could have sold some lower OTM puts and kept holding your short position. Now as the PYPL price moves back up, your puts become less and less valuable as they get closer to expiry. Therefore, you collect the premium whether you decide to buy the puts back at a lower price or let them expire worthless.

As PYPL kept churning up and down, you could have repeatedly sold weekly puts when it got close to the $71.50 level, each time allowing them to expire worthless. Remember these are covered puts, so if the stock drops dramatically as it finally did May 9th, your short put position is not going to destroy your account. This is because you are holding the short position in the shares as well.

Covered Calls and Puts

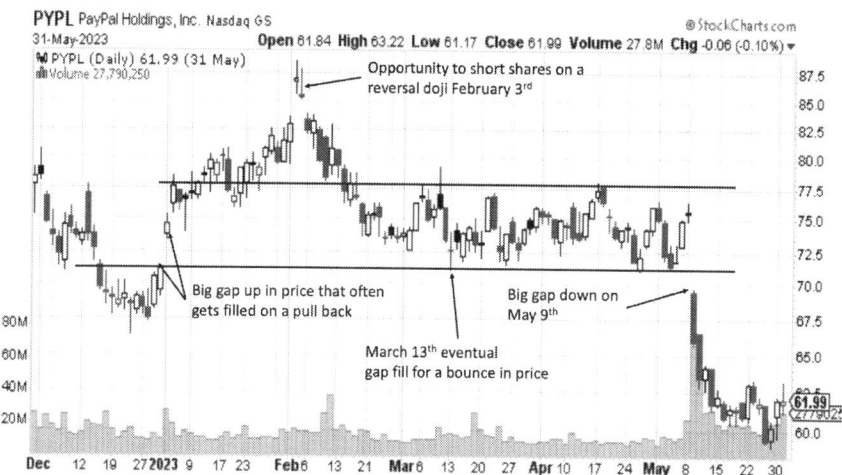

Figure 11.2 Chart of PYPL showing how rangebound price moves can give a trader the opportunity to continue to generate revenue while holding the shares short (chart courtesy of StockCharts.com).

As always, the negative aspect of selling covered options is the risk of eventually having the shares move ITM which limits your gains. The short position is still a winner, but now the puts are a loser once they expire ITM. You need to decide to cover both positions, or if you still feel there is more downside in the shares, buy back the puts for a loss and continue to hold the shares short.

Similar option trading guidelines apply when selling covered calls or puts. Let's conclude this section by reviewing the steps and criteria many traders follow when executing this type of trade:

» While you should consider the underlying security position to have some long-term possibilities for gains, in the shorter term you will generally expect the security to trade in a defined range for a period of time.

» When selling the OTM option, look to obtain at least 1.0% in revenue weekly. The longer the time to expiry that you select, the more premium you will garner due to the time value in the option. This also reflects the higher likelihood that your OTM option may move to be ITM ahead of the expiry date.

- » It is crucial that you monitor your trade. In particular, pay attention to the underlying security price action. Be cognizant of your stop, and honor it if the security does not trade as you had hoped.
- » Give thought to exiting around half of the trade once you are at the 50% profit position. This locks in some profits and you can then permit the rest to run.

CHAPTER SUMMARY

The covered option trading strategy I reviewed in this chapter can be summarized as follows:

- » Generating revenue with existing positions is another way to use options. The strategy is known as a covered call (or put).
- » Covered means that you already have the underlying security in your portfolio. Then, in order to receive the premium to be paid by the call or put buyer, you will either sell an OTM call against your long position, or sell an OTM put against the short position that you are holding. Essentially, you are leveraging your position so that you can collect an additional revenue stream at the option expiry date.
- » One of three things can happen when you are holding the covered option:
    1. the underlying security moves very little, in which case you keep the premium and possibly repeat the process again,
    2. the underlying security moves away from the strike price, in which case you lose on the security holding, but keep the premium on the option you sold, or
    3. the underlying security moves toward and past the strike price, which means you must decide whether to buy back the option or give up the position and bank your profits.

CHAPTER 12

Protecting Positions

I will now discuss a way to protect existing profits on current positions. It is usually employed when you have seen some good gains on your position, and you want to preserve those gains without exiting the position and missing out on further anticipated profits.

To initiate these kinds of positions you need to refer to your charts, conduct some fundamental analysis, and consider whether you want to use one of these strategies. The two strategies I will discuss in the following sections are:

» Purchasing a put or call

» Risk reversal

Purchasing a Put or Call

Purchasing a put or call is one of the most basic strategies you can use to protect your underlying security positions (often referred to as hedging a position). This is essentially buying insurance on your profitable position. Nobody buys insurance because they are expecting a disaster to happen, however they are glad they have it when a bad event occurs.

In implementing this protection plan, do keep in mind that implied volatility (IV) on an underlying security rises and falls based on upcoming events such as an earnings release. Before an earnings release or a comparable significant known event, option prices are elevated as traders presume there will be higher volatility in the price movement of the security. As you will have noticed when trading, the issuance of a news release for this sort of event can cause wild swings in price.

Should you decide to buy a put or call for protection just in advance of this type of an event, you will pay a sizable premium for that option. After the news release, the IV premium in the option you bought is probably going to drop, resulting in a decrease in value for the option you purchased. This reduction may be nullified if the option you chose went ITM. This is when your insurance policy will kick in to protect you from additional losses on your holding.

You can utilize this strategy if you are seeking to safeguard gains going into an event, or for insurance against losing all the gains you have acquired in a position over a period of time. Hedge funds will often use this strategy to shield their profits as it is difficult for them to get into and out of large positions. It is easier for them to buy options as an insurance policy to protect their holdings.

Let's look at a simple example of purchasing a put against a profitable position. Assume you had decided to take a long position on DraftKings Inc (DKNG) on August 3rd 2021 with an entry price of approximately $48.00 per share. You had concluded through your analysis that the stock looked like it had bottomed, and was setting up to move higher after it stayed above the 20-day simple moving average. Figure 12.1 illustrates how this evolved into a very shrewd trade as the price of DKNG marched higher through August and into early September.

However, DKNG did experience a pretty significant price drop September 13th giving you some second thoughts on whether the move higher was done, or if this pullback was just another area of price consolidation before the uptrend continued. At this point you could sell some or all of your position for a nice profit, or you could have bought some puts to protect your gains.

On September 17th, the $56.00 October 15th monthly puts were trading for around $2.00 per contract. Purchasing these puts would have locked in a sale price at the $56.00 level in case the share price of DKNG really started to sell off. Referring to the chart in Figure 12.1, this was a prudent trade as the share price continued to drop significantly and ultimately returned to the original entry of $48.00.

As the DKNG share price dropped, at any time up to expiry you could have sold your puts for a profit and exited the long position on the shares as well keeping most of your gains. Alternatively, if you had held the shares and the puts to expiry on October 15th, the put seller would have been obligated to buy your shares at the $56.00 level with the market price of DKNG closing the day at about the $48.00 price level. Recall that you bought these puts for about $2.00 per contract, so in this case, your net profit is based on a net sale price of $54.00 ($56.00 sale price less the $2.00 cost of the put).

Be aware that if DKNG had remained at roughly the same price or had started to move even higher, the put option you paid $2.00 per share for would have been of no value if held to expiry. Similar to an automobile insurance policy that a driver pays for every year, it is there if you need it but if you are free of accidents, the money you paid is gone. With an option, however, you do have the ability to sell it and not allow the put to expire worthless. You will no doubt be selling it for a lower price as the passage of time erodes its value, but if it seems that you will not require it, then you do have that choice.

Figure 12.1 - Chart of DKNG showing some topping action that might motivate a trader to protect their gains using put options (chart courtesy of StockCharts.com).

Protective puts can be a helpful tool if you expect a possible short to intermediate-term drop in the price of a security that you own, but do not want to sell. In the same manner, protective calls can be used to ensure a profitable short position does not turn against you and become a loser.

Risk Reversals

A risk reversal is another option hedging strategy that you can use to protect your existing positions. When implemented, this strategy will protect against an unfavorable price movement in your position however, it will also limit your profits. Risk reversals are also known as protective collars.

To execute a risk reversal, one option is purchased and then a second option is sold. The option sale helps pay for the cost of the purchased option, and in some cases, the trader actually ends up with a credit in their account with the sale bringing in more money than

Protecting Positions

the cost to purchase. But as you know, nothing is free, and the option sale will limit the profit if the price of the underlying security moves significantly in your favour.

Let's look at an example of how a risk reversal can be implemented to hedge a long position. Referring to Figure 12.2, you will see a chart of META Platforms, Inc. (META) which had a very strong move higher when it broke out on a good earnings report on April 27th, 2023. Another positive report on July 27th sent the stock gapping higher again. But now price action is showing some signs of buyer exhaustion, and it may consolidate for a while by trading in a narrow range. This is an example of where you might consider a risk reversal strategy to stay in the position and protect your gains, if you had been holding META since May.

In this situation you refer to your options chain to view the various prices on the options that are available for a monthly option expiry date. You are expecting some range trading for a while, so you consider using monthly options that expire August 18th, 2023. At the time of writing, a $302.50 put could be bought for $4.00, and at the same time a $325.00 call could be sold for about $4.50.

Buying the put now gives you the right to sell META at $302.50, should the security drop below that level locking in your profit. Selling the call actually put some money in your account ($4.50 call sell less $4.00 put buy = $0.50 or $50.00 on one contract). However, if the price of META stock starts to rally and goes above the $325.00 level, your profit is capped there unless you take some further action such as purchasing the calls back at a higher price.

How to Trade Options

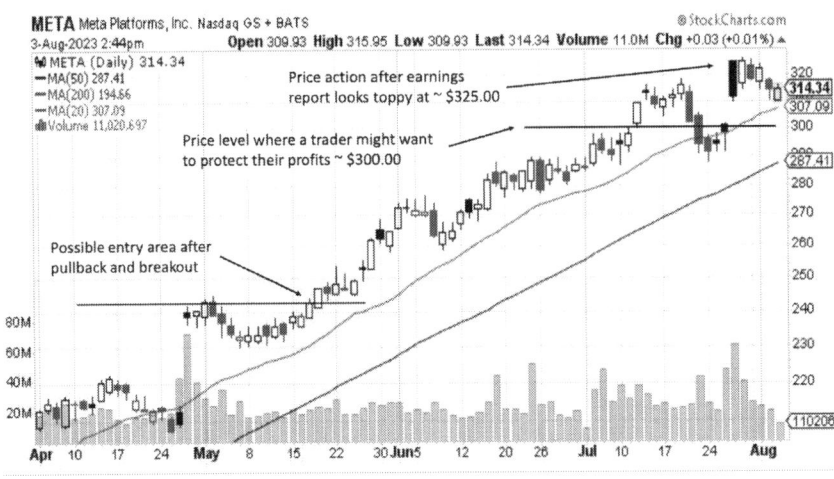

Figure 12.2 Chart of META showing an example of a situation where you might consider using a risk reversal to protect gains (chart courtesy of StockCharts.com).

For illustration purposes, Figure 12.3 shows the option chain that was discussed above, and with the option prices that were available at the time of writing.

Calls								Fri Aug 18 2023	Puts							
Last	Net	Bid	Ask	Vol	IV	Delta	Gamma	Int	Strike	Last	Net	Bid	Ask	Vol	IV	Delta	Gamma	Int
16.04	-0.335	16.25	16.4	45	0.35	0.7275	0.0149	1732	META 302.500	4	-0.125	3.85	3.9	248	0.35	-0.2742	0.015	2193
14.15	-0.475	14.5	14.6	194	0.35	0.6891	0.016	2934	META 305.000	4.61	-0.29	4.55	4.65	695	0.35	-0.3129	0.0161	4481
12.7	-0.3	12.8	12.95	223	0.34	0.6481	0.0169	377	META 307.500	5.63	-0.12	5.4	5.45	161	0.34	-0.3543	0.0171	2929
11.35	-0.1	11.25	11.35	634	0.34	0.6048	0.0177	19342	META 310.000	6.35	-0.35	6.3	6.4	912	0.34	-0.3981	0.0179	16061
9.9	-0.15	9.85	9.9	551	0.34	0.5598	0.0182	1281	META 312.500	7.4	-0.4	7.35	7.45	440	0.34	-0.4436	0.0185	886
8.65	-0.1	8.5	8.6	1,524	0.34	0.5139	0.0185	4186	META 315.000	8.8	-0.2	8.55	8.65	957	0.34	-0.4901	0.0188	3613
7.25	-0.35	7.3	7.4	360	0.33	0.4677	0.0186	1229	META 317.500	9.92	-0.43	9.85	9.95	385	0.33	-0.537	0.0188	890
6.35	-0.175	6.25	6.35	630	0.33	0.422	0.0183	6020	META 320.000	11.35	-0.45	11.3	11.4	319	0.33	-0.5835	0.0187	2332
5.3	-0.3	5.3	5.4	346	0.33	0.3775	0.0179	1493	META 322.500	13.2	-0.15	12.85	12.95	214	0.33	-0.6289	0.0182	890
4.51	-0.215	4.45	4.55	595	0.33	0.3348	0.0171	4117	META 325.000	15	-0.025	14.5	14.65	114	0.33	-0.6725	0.0175	1144

Figure 12.3 Options chain table of META showing price levels to execute the risk reversal trade (table courtesy of www.cboe.com).

Protecting Positions

Risk reversals can be done for short positions as well. Assume you are short a security and it has been going down but seems to be finding a bottom. You believe this is a temporary pause and the stock price is ultimately going to head lower, but you want to protect your profits. To execute a risk reversal trade in this situation, you would buy a higher OTM call and finance that by selling a lower priced OTM put.

Holding the call allows you to buy the shares and cover your position and take profits if the stock price reverses and goes higher. Selling the put finances the call purchase, but it will become a liability should the security continue to head lower. Figure 12.4 shows a chart of International Business Machines (IBM) where you could have used a risk reversal trade.

Figure 12.4 Chart of IBM showing an example of a situation where you might consider using a risk reversal to protect gains on the short side (chart courtesy of StockCharts.com).

In this situation, you may have been concerned that IBM was doing a double bottom and ready to reverse trend after catching a good short entry on a gap fill at around $134.00. Picking a call strike price of $126.00 would be an area you could consider to take profits, because a close above there would confirm a possible reverse in trend.

You would therefore buy a $126 call in case you need to cover your short position and finance that purchase by selling, let's say, a $120 put. As it turns out in this case, IBM did break above the $126.00 price, possibly taking you out of your position, but still with a nice profit from the $134.00 short entry.

Protection Summary

In summary, let's discuss why a trader would not just sell a long position on a security if they feel it will go down in price, or cover a short position if they think the price is going to rise. Here are three reasons why protective options can be more appropriate than exiting a position:

1. You are concerned that you will exit too early and then get back too soon on a potential pullback.

2. You see the long-term prospects for a security as being good, but in the short term you sense it may be due for a pullback.

3. For a long position, you hold stock that you have acquired through either a company benefit program or private placement. In certain cases, you could be restricted from selling the shares for a period of time, so you choose to use options to "lock in" the selling price of those shares at a later date.

In order to protect your gains on an existing position in the above situations, a protective option would be considered more attractive than a straightforward position exit.

CHAPTER SUMMARY

The two option trading strategies for protecting profits (hedging) that I reviewed in this chapter can be summarized as follows:

» The first strategy involved simply purchasing a put or a call. This strategy is usually employed when you have seen some good gains on your position, and you want to preserve those gains without exiting the position and missing out on further anticipated profits.

» Buying an OTM put is essentially an insurance policy that can be used to protect upside gains from being lost. Conversely, buying an OTM call can be used to protect a short position that has been very profitable.

» A risk reversal is another option hedging strategy that you can use to protect your existing positions.

» To execute a risk reversal, one option is purchased and then a second option is sold. The sale of the one option pays or partially pays for the purchase of the other option.

» To execute a risk reversal strategy with a long position, you would sell a OTM call at a higher strike price compared to the underlying security. You would then buy a OTM put with a strike price below the current security price. You are now protected if your long position drops in price, but you have capped your potential profits if the security rises above the call strike price.

» To execute a risk reversal strategy with a short position, you would sell a OTM put at a lower strike price compared to the underlying security. You would then buy a OTM call with a strike price above the current security price. You are now protected if your short position goes up in price, but you have capped your potential profits if the security drops below the put strike price.

CHAPTER 13
Straddles and Strangles

In this chapter we will discuss several more advanced option strategies called straddles and strangles. When considering implementing these more complex trades, it is important to have a good understanding of what your positions will do under different conditions.

Similar to some of the options strategies we have already discussed, straddles and strangles involve taking a combination of two option trades. These combinations are used when a trader believes that the price of the underlying security is going to move significantly one way or the other, but they are not certain which way it will go. That means a trader that uses this strategy is "directionally agnostic". They do not care which direction the underlying security moves, as long as it moves a lot.

Traders often use this trade strategy just before a company's earnings report or possibly around the time of another known news release. Maybe it is a drug company that is about to announce the results of a drug trial that could have a significant impact on the valuation of that company.

In the following two sections I will discuss both strategies and how they can be used to make potentially profitable trades while limiting your risk as a buyer of the options. I will end the chapter by looking at these trades as a seller.

Straddles

A straddle is an option strategy that involves buying a put and a call of an underlying security at the same strike and the same expiry date. When you buy an ATM put and call, the net delta should be close to zero, because the positive delta of the call is negated by the negative delta of the put. That means a dollar move in the price of the underlying security will have a positive impact on one option and an equivalent negative impact on the other.

However, as the underlying price increasingly moves in one direction, the option that is ITM continues to move higher approaching a delta of almost 1.0 for a call and -1.0 for a put (every dollar move in the underlying is another dollar move in the option). Meanwhile the OTM option approaches zero which is your maximum loss on that portion of the trade. The trader's hope is that the ITM option gain ends up being a multiple of the loss suffered on the OTM option.

Let's look at an example using Apple Inc.'s (AAPL) earnings report that occurred August 3, 2023. Figure 13.1 shows an option chain table with the prices of AAPL options just before their earnings release. At the close before the release, AAPL was trading around $192.00. The closest strike price to the current underlying stock price is $192.50. Therefore, you could have bought a $192.50 call for $3.08 per contract and a put option for $3.75 per contract. Not a perfect one for one, but you have to expect to pay a little more for one contract compared to the other, because the underlying security price is not usually right at the strike prices offered.

Straddles and Strangles

Options Chain
Option chain of AAPL just before earnings release on August 3, 2023
Total Records: 2

Calls									Fri Aug 04 2023	Puts								
Last	Net	Bid	Ask	Vol	IV	Delta	Gamma	Int	Strike	Last	Net	Bid	Ask	Vol	IV	Delta	Gamma	Int
7.7	-0.975	7.8	7.85	908	0.83	0.7928	0.0328	2741	AAPL 185.000	1.02	+0.225	1.02	1.03	18,605	0.83	-0.2073	0.0328	15095
5.93	-0.82	5.95	6.05	1,365	0.82	0.7	0.0401	1777	AAPL 187.500	1.69	+0.335	1.68	1.69	12,089	0.83	-0.3001	0.0401	10600
4.45	-0.575	4.4	4.45	6,765	0.83	0.5922	0.045	13162	AAPL 190.000	2.61	+0.45	2.6	2.61	24,194	0.83	-0.408	0.045	31691
3.08	-0.545	3.05	3.1	19,212	0.81	0.477	0.0467	14157	AAPL 192.500	3.75	+0.525	3.75	3.8	8,362	0.82	-0.5233	0.0467	13580
1.99	-0.47	1.98	1.99	24,892	0.79	0.3611	0.0448	43120	AAPL 195.000	5.17	+0.595	5.15	5.2	4,620	0.79	-0.6393	0.0449	17691
1.17	-0.385	1.17	1.18	17,176	0.77	0.252	0.0394	20355	AAPL 197.500	6.9	+0.75	6.8	6.9	926	0.76	-0.7487	0.0394	5986

AAPL trading close to $192.00 therefore $192.50 is the closest strike price
Purchase call at $3.08 and purchase put at $3.75

Figure 13.1 Options chain table of AAPL showing prices available to use a straddle strategy just before the earnings report is released (table courtesy of www.Cboe.com).

Now with the benefit of hindsight, let's look at how this trade worked out. AAPL earnings were released, and overall, the results disappointed traders and investors. The stock sold off on April 4th and closed the day at a price of around $182.00, which was a bigger price move compared to what was expected.

In fact, by looking at the price of the put and call at or near the strike price, you can easily calculate the move that is expected by the option markets. In AAPL's case the expected move was about $7.00 ($3.08 plus $3.75 = ~ $7.00), or $3.50 on either side of the current price. The move of $10.00 down was much larger than the market expected, so this straddle trade would have worked out very well if you had used this strategy.

Referring to Figure 13.2, you can see the option chain table of AAPL after the earnings report at the end of the trading day. While the AAPL calls that were bought at $3.09 would have been worthless, the put options went from $3.75 to close at $10.50. That is a $6.75 gain on the puts, and a loss of $3.09 on the calls, resulting in a $3.66 profit on the straddle trade (before commissions). That is about a 50% gain on that trade – not bad for a day's work.

Options chain of AAPL just after the earnings release on August 3, 2023

Calls									Fri Aug 04 2023 ∧	Puts								
Last	Net	Bid	Ask	Vol	IV	Delta	Gamma	Int	Strike	Last	Net	Bid	Ask	Vol	IV	Delta	Gamma	Int
14.65	-8.975	13.7	15.3	248	3.98	0.9985	0.001	113	AAPL 167.500	0.01	-0.045	0	0.01	181	4.03	-0.0015	0.001	11852
12.4	-8.75	11.6	12.8	1,339	3.33	0.9982	0.0014	1382	AAPL 170.000	0.01	-0.075	0	0.01	2,140	3.38	-0.0018	0.0014	31227
9.7	-8.975	9	10.3	492	2.68	0.9977	0.0021	194	AAPL 172.500	0.01	-0.095	0	0.01	1,316	2.72	-0.0023	0.0021	7651
7.01	-9.215	6.2	7.8	784	2.03	0.9969	0.0036	696	AAPL 175.000	0.01	-0.145	0	0.01	4,682	2.05	-0.0031	0.0036	14192
4.65	-9.15	3.75	5.3	963	1.36	0.9954	0.0077	295	AAPL 177.500	0.01	-0.225	0	0.01	7,007	1.38	-0.0046	0.0077	9867
2	-9.45	1.76	2.27	4,521	0.88	0.9904	0.0299	3636	AAPL 180.000	0.01	-0.375	0	0.01	42,340	0.68	-0.0096	0.0299	43272
0.01	-9.24	0	0.01	26,247	0.21	0.1613	0.481	1830	AAPL 182.500	0.48	-0.195	0.48	0.55	107,929	0	-0.8387	0.481	15296
0.01	-7.215	0	0.01	103,583	0.95	0.0068	0.0158	2486	AAPL 185.000	3.03	+1.875	2.97	3.1	117,484	0	-0.9932	0.0158	23975
0.01	-5.465	0	0.01	129,933	1.61	0.0041	0.006	1739	AAPL 187.500	5.55	+3.665	5.2	5.85	36,056	0	-0.9959	0.006	14837
0.01	-3.965	0	0.01	107,158	2.22	0.003	0.0032	17961	AAPL 190.000	8.05	+5.18	7.95	8.8	39,431	0	-0.997	0.0032	32275
0.01	-2.675	0	0.01	33,799	2.82	0.0024	0.0021	22041	AAPL 192.500	10.5	+6.4	10.45	11.3	8,855	0	-0.9976	0.0021	13680
0.01	-1.685	0	0.01	17,057	3.39	0.002	0.0014	46986	AAPL 195.000	12.95	+7.325	12.55	13.65	5,493	0	-0.998	0.0014	15782

AAPL closes at $182.00. The $192.50 call expires worthless while the $192.50 put sells at $10.50 netting a nice profit on the trade

Figure 13.2 Options chain table of AAPL showing the trading prices of the $192.50 options after the earnings report was released (table courtesy of www.Cboe.com).

Obviously, for a straddle strategy to work like this AAPL example, you need to have a big move in the underlying security after the event. If AAPL had reported marginally better results, maybe traders and investors would not have been inclined to sell the stock price down.

In the scenario where the AAPL price had remained close to its pre-earnings release price of $192.00, the price of both the put and call options would have dropped, and you would not have had a winning trade to offset the losing trade. Both options would have dropped in price which is called an "IV crush".

This IV crush refers to the drop in implied volatility (IV) that happens after the event has passed and the outcome is public knowledge. The IV drop is especially severe if it turns out to be an inconsequential event. An example of such an event could be an earnings report that meets, but does not exceed or disappoint the expectations of the market players.

This lack of price movement and the associated IV crush is the risk you are exposed to should you decide to use this straddle strategy. However, because you are purchasing the put and call options, your risk is defined. The worst-case scenario, if you take no further action, is that both options will go to zero at expiry. However, you may be able to get some of your money back by selling them before they expire worthless.

Now that you understand the straddle, let's compare this strategy to a strangle in the following section.

Strangle

A strangle is similar to a straddle in that a trader has the expectation that the price of the underlying security is going to move significantly one way or the other, but is not certain which way it will go. Once again, a trader that uses the strangle strategy is "directionally agnostic". They do not care which direction the underlying security moves, as long as it moves a lot.

Using a strangle strategy involves buying a put and a call option that are OTM. A lot of traders will use options with roughly the same delta so a put may have a delta of -0.20 and a call may have a +0.20. The advantage of a strangle is that it is a cheaper trade to execute compared to the straddle, because the ATM options are more expensive in comparison to the OTM options. The trade-off for getting the cheaper options is that the underlying security price will need to move more for the trade to payoff.

Let's look at an example using the same AAPL earnings report on August 3, 2023. In the case of a strangle, before the earnings release you could buy an OTM $185.00 strike price put for $1.02 with a delta of -0.21. Next you could buy an OTM $197.50 strike price call for $1.17 with a delta of 0.25, which is fairly close to your put values. Refer to the option chain table in Figure 13.3 with AAPL trading at $192.00 at the close of the trading day.

Option chain of AAPL just before earnings release on August 3, 2023

Options Chain　　　　　　　　　　　　　　　　　　　　　　　　　Total Records: 24

Calls　　　　　　　　　　　　　Fri Aug 04 2023　　**Puts**

Last	Net	Bid	Ask	Vol	IV	Delta	Gamma	Int	Strike	Last	Net	Bid	Ask	Vol	IV	Delta	Gamma	Int
7.7	-0.975	7.8	7.85	908	0.83	0.7928	0.0328	2741	AAPL 185.000	1.02	+0.225	1.02	1.03	18,605	0.83	-0.2073	0.0328	15095
5.93	-0.82	5.95	6.05	1,365	0.82	0.7	0.0401	1777	AAPL 187.500	1.69	+0.335	1.68	1.69	12,089	0.83	-0.3001	0.0401	10600
4.45	-0.575	4.4	4.45	6,765	0.83	0.5922	0.045	13162	AAPL 190.000	2.61	+0.45	2.6	2.61	24,194	0.83	-0.408	0.045	31691
3.08	-0.545	3.05	3.1	19,212	0.81	0.477	0.0467	14157	AAPL 192.500	3.75	+0.525	3.75	3.8	8,362	0.82	-0.5233	0.0467	13580
1.99	-0.47	1.98	1.99	24,892	0.79	0.3611	0.0448	43120	AAPL 195.000	5.17	+0.595	5.15	5.2	4,620	0.79	-0.6393	0.0449	17691
1.17	-0.385	1.17	1.18	17,176	0.77	0.252	0.0394	20355	AAPL 197.500	6.9	+0.75	6.8	6.9	926	0.76	-0.7487	0.0394	5986

AAPL price is close to $192.00 at the end of the day. You could initiate a strangle by purchasing an OTM $197.50 call for $1.17 and purchasing an OTM $185.00 put for $1.02

Figure 13.3 Options chain table of AAPL showing prices available to use a strangle strategy just before the earnings report is released (Table courtesy of www.Cboe.com).

Now you wait for the earnings release and hope for a large price move one way or the other. Remember, you do not care which way it moves as long as it moves a lot. Figure 13.4 shows how your options traded after earnings. You can see that due to the relatively large drop in the price of AAPL to $182.00, your OTM puts went up and finished the day at $3.03, while the calls expired worthless (not shown on the table but the strike price was a long way OTM at expiry).

Options chain of AAPL just after the earnings release on August 3, 2023

Calls　　　　　　　　　　　　　Fri Aug 04 2023　　**Puts**

Last	Net	Bid	Ask	Vol	IV	Delta	Gamma	Int	Strike	Last	Net	Bid	Ask	Vol	IV	Delta	Gamma	Int
14.65	-8.975	13.7	15.3	248	3.98	0.9985	0.001	113	AAPL 167.500	0.01	-0.045	0	0.01	181	4.03	-0.0015	0.001	11852
12.4	-8.75	11.6	12.8	1,339	3.33	0.9982	0.0014	1382	AAPL 170.000	0.01	-0.075	0	0.01	2,140	3.38	-0.0018	0.0014	31227
9.7	-8.975	9	10.3	492	2.68	0.9977	0.0021	194	AAPL 172.500	0.01	-0.095	0	0.01	1,316	2.72	-0.0023	0.0021	7651
7.01	-9.215	6.2	7.8	784	2.03	0.9969	0.0036	696	AAPL 175.000	0.01	-0.145	0	0.01	4,682	2.05	-0.0031	0.0036	14192
4.65	-9.15	3.75	5.3	963	1.36	0.9954	0.0077	295	AAPL 177.500	0.01	-0.225	0	0.01	7,008	1.38	-0.0046	0.0077	9867
2	-9.45	1.76	2.27	4,521	0.88	0.9904	0.0299	3636	AAPL 180.000	0.01	-0.375	0	0.01	42,340	0.68	-0.0096	0.0299	43272
0.01	-9.24	0	0.01	26,247	0.21	0.1613	0.481	1830	AAPL 182.500	0.48	-0.195	0.48	0.55	107,929	0	-0.8387	0.481	15296
0.01	-7.215	0	0.01	103,583	0.95	0.0068	0.0158	2486	AAPL 185.000	3.03	+1.875	2.97	3.1	117,484	0	-0.9932	0.0158	23975
0.01	-5.465	0	0.01	129,933	1.61	0.0041	0.006	1739	AAPL 187.500	5.55	+3.665	5.2	5.85	36,056	0	-0.9959	0.006	14837
0.01	-3.965	0	0.01	107,158	2.22	0.003	0.0032	17961	AAPL 190.000	8.05	+5.18	7.95	8.8	39,431	0	-0.997	0.0032	32275
0.01	-2.675	0	0.01	33,799	2.82	0.0024	0.0021	22041	AAPL 192.500	10.5	+6.4	10.45	11.3	8,855	0	-0.9976	0.0021	13680
0.01	-1.685	0	0.01	17,057	3.39	0.002	0.0014	46986	AAPL 195.000	12.95	+7.325	12.55	13.65	5,493	0	-0.998	0.0014	15782

AAPL closes at $182.00. The $197.50 call expire worthless while the $185.00 put sells at $3.03 netting a nice profit on the trade

Figure 13.4 Options chain table of AAPL showing the trading prices of the $185.00 put option and the $197.50 call after the earnings report was released (table courtesy of www.Cboe.com).

In this case, the strangle was also profitable. The trade cost a total of $2.19 which is the sum of the cost of the put and call options ($1.02 plus $1.17). The OTM call expired worthless if held to expiry that day, however the sale of the OTM put option collected you $3.03 resulting in a profit of $0.84 which is about a 38% return on your investment. Note that this profit will be a little less because it does not account for commissions.

Straddles Versus Strangles

As it is with many trading strategies, the one you choose to use often depends on your personal objectives, financial situation, and risk tolerance. A straddle will cost you more because ATM options are more expensive, however its value will begin to rise as soon as there is a price move in the underlying security. In comparison, the strangle is cheaper to execute, however the value will not start to rise until the underlying security price starts to get close to the strike price of one of the OTM options you bought.

Remember, you do not need to hold options to expiry. Many options traders will close out their positions immediately after the event has passed because of the element of time decay that happens when an option approaches expiry (theta).

The main risk in using the straddle or strangle strategy is that the price move in the underlying security may not be enough, after the event, to compensate for the cost of executing the trades. The IV value tells you what traders are thinking about when it comes to the expected move once the event happens.

The higher the IV, the more you will pay for the options because traders are pricing in the potential for a big price move one way or the other. You can compare current IV percentiles to previous IV values as a gauge of where the IV value is for this current upcoming event. This does not mean you should not trade a security with a high IV. Just understand you will be paying more for the options.

Holding a straddle or strangle through an event is a double-edged sword. If you get a large price move beyond what is expected, your trade will likely be profitable. If there is not a lot of response to the event and price action is subdued, implied volatility will naturally drop (IV crush) taking the price of the options down with it. That leaves you with two unprofitable positions that you will have to close for a loss, which could be significant on a percentage basis.

Straddles and Strangles Short Plays

As with all options trades you can be the buyer or the seller. So far in this chapter we have discussed the strategy that involves being the buyer, but you can also use this strategy as a seller. You would take the position as a seller of both options if you believed that the price of the underlying security was not going to move a lot after a known event.

Recalling chapter 9 where we discussed selling options, the upside for the trade sees the seller keep all the money they collected from the sale. The negative outcome is that you could lose many times the amount you collect if you are wrong and the options you sold move well ITM.

If we use the AAPL example discussed earlier in the chapter, you can see that in this case, if you had been the seller of those positions, you would have lost money because AAPL moved more than the market had expected. This is the challenge you face when trading based on the outcome of an event. It is somewhat akin to betting on the outcome of a spin on a roulette wheel. However, there are traders that feel they can get it right more often than being wrong.

Of course, you can always find a way to make options trades even more complex, by using spread strategies around the current price, to limit the amount you will lose if you're wrong. These vertical spread strategies were discussed in chapter 10. When used to trade around an event and applied to both sides of a security price they have names like "iron condor" and "iron butterfly". These two strategies are executed as follows:

1. **Iron Condor** – Selling an OTM put and call option with strike prices close to the current price (short strangle) then buying a put and call further OTM to protect from large losses.

2. **Iron Butterfly** – Selling an ATM put and call option with a strike price ATM (short straddle) then buying a put and call OTM to protect from large losses.

The iron condor and iron butterfly essentially combine two different options into one options position setup. The vertical trades have the disadvantage of lowering the potential profit, because you need to use some of the proceeds of the higher priced options sales to purchase further OTM options for protection against unlimited losses.

Let's look at how an iron butterfly would have performed with the AAPL earnings release shown in Figure 13.5. With AAPL trading at around $192.50, you could have sold the ATM call and collect $308.00 per contract and also sold the put at the same strike price for $375.00. You have collected a total of $683.00 (not including commission cost). However, you want protection in case AAPL makes a big move after earnings, so you buy an OTM $187.50 put at a cost of $169.00 and a $197.50 call for a cost of $117.00. These trades cost you a total of $286.00 which means the net amount you brought into your account was just under $400.00 (collecting $683.00 for selling the options less the $286.00 for purchasing the protective options).

Option chain of AAPL just before earnings release on August 3, 2023

Options Chain — AAPL trading close to $192.00 therefore $192.50 is the closest strike price; sell a put at $3.75 and purchase an OTM put at $1.69   Total Records: 2

Calls									Fri Aug 04 2023	Puts								
Last	Net	Bid	Ask	Vol	IV	Delta	Gamma	Int	Strike	Last	Net	Bid	Ask	Vol	IV	Delta	Gamma	Int
7.7	-0.975	7.8	7.85	908	0.83	0.7928	0.0328	2741	AAPL 185.000	1.02	+0.225	1.02	1.03	18,605	0.83	-0.2073	0.0328	15095
5.93	-0.82	5.95	6.05	1,365	0.82	0.7	0.0401	1777	AAPL 187.500	1.69	+0.335	1.68	1.69	12,089	0.83	-0.3001	0.0401	10600
4.45	-0.575	4.4	4.45	6,765	0.83	0.5922	0.045	13162	AAPL 190.000	2.61	+0.45	2.6	2.61	24,194	0.83	-0.408	0.045	31691
3.08	-0.545	3.05	3.1	19,212	0.81	0.477	0.0467	14157	AAPL 192.500	3.75	+0.525	3.75	3.8	8,362	0.82	-0.5233	0.0467	13580
1.99	-0.47	1.98	1.99	24,892	0.79	0.3611	0.0448	43120	AAPL 195.000	5.17	+0.595	5.15	5.2	4,620	0.79	-0.6393	0.0449	17691
1.17	-0.385	1.17	1.18	17,176	0.77	0.252	0.0394	20355	AAPL 197.500	6.9	+0.75	6.8	6.9	926	0.76	-0.7487	0.0394	5986

AAPL trading close to $192.00 therefore $192.50 is the closest strike price; sell a call at $3.08 and purchase an OTM call at $1.17

Figure 13.5 Table showing the options prices you would have been working with before the AAPL earnings release (table courtesy of Cboe.com)

Now you sit back and hope that the AAPL price does not move much after the earnings. Unfortunately, for this trade, AAPL moved a lot after earnings and the results of the trade can be seen back in Table 13.1. The options prices after the news release can be viewed back in Figure 13.4 and you can see that this trade did result in a small loss. However, the downside protection you had with the purchase of the OTM put saved the trade from being a much bigger loser than it would have been without the protective put.

Position	Credit/Debit before news	Value after news	Result of trades
Short $192.50 call	+$308.00	$0.00	+$308.00
Long $197.50 call	-$117.00	$0.00	-$117.00
Short $192.50 put	+$375.00	+$1050.00	-$675.00 (you were short so it's a loss)
Long $187.50 put	-$169.00	+$555.00	+$386.00
Net	+ $398.00		-$98.00

Table 13.1 The results of an iron condor options trade that could have been executed prior to the AAPL earnings release. It shows that buying an OTM put option significantly limited the loss a trader would have otherwise realized without that protection.

In summary, there are multiple approaches using options to play earnings releases or other known upcoming news events. The strategy you choose to take is going to depend on many factors including market conditions, your assessment of a securities current value and prospects, your financial situation, personal financial objectives and risk tolerance.

There is another way to trade off of earnings results which I feel is less risky. I will discuss that alternative strategy later in the book.

CHAPTER SUMMARY

In this chapter I discussed several options strategies that can be used to play known upcoming events that might impact the price of the underlying security. The summary is as follows:

» Traders will often use trade strategies called a straddle and strangle just before a company's earnings report or around the time of another known news release.

» Traders have an expectation that the price of the underlying security is going to move significantly one way or the other, but they are not certain which way it will go. That means the trader is "directionally agnostic"

» A straddle is an options strategy that involves buying a put and a call of an underlying security at the same strike and the same expiry date. The strike price chosen is one that is as close as possible to the current price before the news event.

» If the straddle trade strategy is executed and there is a subsequent large price move in the underlying security, one option will dramatically increase in price while the other option will approach zero. The holder is hoping the gain in one option is many times more than the loss on the other.

- » If the price does not move significantly as hoped, both options will drop in price putting the trader in a loss position. The maximum loss is limited to the cost of the two options.
- » A strangle is an options strategy that involves buying a put and a call of an underlying security at different strike prices but with the same expiry date. Both put and call options strike prices are OTM by about the same amount compared to the current price.
- » The strangle costs less to execute compared to the straddle, however the price of the underlying security needs to move more for the trade to be profitable, and profits may not be as good as we saw with our AAPL example.
- » Traders can take the opposite side of the trade and become the seller of straddles and strangles, but they are taking on more risk as the seller.
- » To limit losses as an options seller, vertical spreads can be used in the case of both straddles and strangles. These are referred to as an "iron condor" and "iron butterfly".

CHAPTER 14
Stock Replacement Strategy

In the following couple of chapters I will discuss a number of trade situations where you can utilize one or more of the options trade strategies that I covered in the previous chapters of the book.

As was discussed earlier, options can be used for day trading, swing, and longer-term position trading. You can consider these various setups and decide if one or more of them might work for you given your financial situation, risk tolerance, and the type of trading you prefer.

I have chosen to break these setups into individual chapters to make it easier for you to differentiate between the setups, and allow you to easily focus on the ideas that might fit your trade preferences. This chapter will cover two topics as follows:

» Stock replacement
» Risk reversal revisited

Stock Replacement

The first trade setup we will examine is also one of the most straight-forward. It is referred to as a stock replacement strategy. It involves using options to take a position in an underlying security instead of purchasing that same security.

This is a strategy typically used by a swing trader or a trader with a longer-term view. In the case of swing trading or longer-term investing, you would have identified a security that you felt was likely to trend higher in price over an extended period of time. Instead of purchasing the security directly, you would purchase an ITM call. For this strategy, many options traders like to use a strike price that is "deep" ITM (well away from the current market price).

The reason you buy the deep ITM calls is because these options will have a delta of very close to one. This means that every one dollar move higher in the underlying security results in an equivalent one dollar move in the options. Therefore, owning these ITM options is very similar to owning the security itself in terms of movement in price. This is why it is referred to as a stock replacement strategy.

Let's consider a simple example to illustrate how the leverage effect amplifies the gains seen by the options holder compared to the security holder. In August 2023, AAPL had just reported earnings and pulled back significantly off its all-time high price of $195.00 as can be seen in the chart (Figure 14.1). It is now trading at around $179.00 dollars, and you would like to own the shares because you believe this pullback is a great opportunity to get long. You could buy 100 shares which would cost you about $17,900.00.

Figure 14.1 Chart showing the pricing move on AAPL after earnings and how it finds support at an area it broke out from in June 2023 (chart courtesy of StockCharts.com).

Alternatively, you could use a stock replacement strategy by purchasing a call that is ITM, with a delta close to one, and an expiry date long enough to allow AAPL to recover from the earnings report and move back up again. Going out to the November monthly expiry date, you can buy a $160.00 call expiring on the 17th of the month. This call option would cost you about $24.56 per contract or about $2,456.00 plus commission.

The associated options table is shown in Figure 14.2. You will notice that the delta on this option is about 0.84, meaning every dollar move back up on AAPL will give you a $0.84 gain on the options holding.

Option chain of AAPL after the earnings release on August 3, 2023

Options Chain — Total Records: 10

Calls									Fri Nov 17 2023	Puts							
Last	Net	Bid	Ask	Vol	IV	Delta	Gamma	Int	Strike	Last	Net	Bid	Ask	Vol	IV	Delta Gamma	Int
28.54	+0.865	28.65	28.9	6	0.29	0.8752	0.0076	1007	AAPL 155.000	1.81	-0.18	1.81	1.85	537	0.29	-0.1282 0.0077	4877
24.56	+1.11	24.35	24.6	586	0.28	0.8362	0.0096	3298	AAPL 160.000	2.43	-0.23	2.44	2.46	547	0.28	-0.1684 0.0098	7394
20.35	+0.9	20.3	20.5	71	0.27	0.7865	0.0117	2677	AAPL 165.000	3.29	-0.285	3.25	3.35	222	0.26	-0.2197 0.0121	7239
16.61	+0.885	16.45	16.7	336	0.26	0.7248	0.014	3427	AAPL 170.000	4.47	-0.355	4.4	4.5	1,021	0.25	-0.2839 0.0146	8508
13.3	+0.925	13.05	13.25	820	0.25	0.6514	0.0161	6152	AAPL 175.000	5.96	-0.44	5.9	6	2,197	0.24	-0.3614 0.017	8348
10.05	+0.675	10	10.1	4,544	0.24	0.5677	0.0177	13978	AAPL 180.000	7.85	-0.575	7.8	7.9	4,171	0.23	-0.4513 0.0191	19407
7.44	+0.565	7.35	7.45	598	0.23	0.4775	0.0185	9846	AAPL 185.000	10.15	-0.8	10.2	10.3	268	0.23	-0.5508 0.0206	8471
5.3	+0.425	5.2	5.3	713	0.22	0.3861	0.0183	21369	AAPL 190.000	13	-1.025	13.05	13.25	113	0.22	-0.6556 0.0211	16049
3.65	+0.325	3.55	3.65	560	0.22	0.2994	0.017	18128	AAPL 195.000	16.75	-0.975	16.6	16.8	24	0.21	-0.7602 0.0208	12530
2.41	+0.19	2.4	2.41	2,141	0.21	0.2227	0.0148	17398	AAPL 200.000	20.6	-1.325	20.65	21.5	2	0.22	-0.8599 0.0197	3684

AAPL trading price is close to $179.00 on August 8th – apply a stock replacement strategy by purchasing an deep ITM call for a cost of $24.56 instead of buying AAPL shares

Figure 14.2 Options table showing the pricing on a deep ITM call used for a stock replacement strategy (table courtesy of www.cboe.com).

Now if the price of AAPL does start to move higher, your options position is going to offer a much better rate of return compared to the trader that simply purchased the shares. A 5.00 move up on AAPL shares is going to give you a return of about 2.8%. On the options position you will see a return of about 17% for the same $5.00 move ($5.00 move times delta of 0.84 equals an increase of $4.20 on price of the option which is $420 on the contract of 100 shares). This again illustrates the power of leverage that options offer.

How to Trade Options

Be aware, there are several downsides to this strategy. First, there is no assurance that your assessment on the future direction of the security price is correct. If the security moves in the opposite direction to what you had expected, your losses will also be magnified on a percentage basis.

Do not forget about theta which is not your friend in this trade strategy. You are paying an excess amount of money for the option over the current price which is called the extrinsic value. In our example, you own the $160.00 calls and the stock is trading around $179.00. The difference is $19.00 but you paid $24.56 for the option. If the stock does not move much after your options purchase, the extrinsic value of $5.56 ($24.56-$19.00) will slowly erode as the expiry date draws closer.

Recalling from our discussion about theta in chapter 4, theta erodes slowly when the expiry is more than 60 days away. However, as expiry approaches 30 to 20 days away, this loss in options value starts to accelerate rapidly. This is why you need to closely monitor your position in this trade. If AAPL does not start to move back up in a timely fashion as you had hoped, you may want to exit your position, or at the very least, reduce your holding size to limit your potential loss.

Risk Reversal Revisited

In chapter 12 I discussed a way to protect existing profits on current positions called a risk reversal. This option trade setup can also be employed in the stock replacement strategy that we just discussed.

As you are aware, you will pay an extra amount for a deep ITM call or put when implementing a risk reversal called the extrinsic value. One way to offset the extra amount you will pay for a bullish bet is to sell a higher strike price OTM call to reduce the cost of purchasing the ITM call.

The money you take in on the sale of the call will reduce the amount the stock needs to rise for your trade to become profitable. Of course, the downside on selling this call is that it will cap your gains if you

Stock Replacement Strategy

do see a subsequent strong move higher in price and the OTM call ends up going ITM before the expiry date.

You can apply this same strategy on a security that you feel bearish on by purchasing a deep ITM put then selling a lower strike price OTM put to reduce the cost of the overall trade.

Please review chapter 12 where I discussed in depth this strategy with an example trade if you need a refresher on this setup. The bottom line is that it can also be employed when you do not have a current position in the underlying security.

CHAPTER SUMMARY

The stock replacement strategy can be summarized as follows:

- » This strategy offers a cheaper way to make more profitable returns from a price move on an underlying security without owning the actual shares.
- » You are making a directional bet when using this straight-forward strategy.
- » This is a strategy typically used by a swing trader or a trader with a longer-term view.
- » For a long trade, instead of purchasing a security directly, you purchase a "deep ITM" call option. These deep ITM options typically have a delta that is close to 1.0 so every dollar price move in the underlying security almost equates to the same dollar price move in the options.
- » This strategy can also be employed when a trader has a negative view on the future price of a security. Purchasing deep ITM put options implies you are bearish and expect the stock to drop further and the put to increase in price.
- » The one downside of the strategy is that losses can be magnified if the trade does not work out as planned, just as gains are magnified if the trade works out as hoped.

» As with all options trades, you cannot forget about theta and the decay in options value that occurs as the expiry date approaches. Be prepared to exit if the trade is not working and expiry is drawing near.

» A risk reversal trade setup was also discussed in this chapter as a way to lower the cost of buying deep ITM put or call for a stock replacement play. The downside of selling that OTM put or call is that it will cap your potential gains.

CHAPTER 15
Earnings Plays

In this chapter I will discuss earnings plays. Earnings releases represent a very good opportunity to use options to make a profit because IV is usually elevated due to a possible value changing event for the company.

There are a number of ways to trade the earnings release of a company which can be categorized into two segments:

» Pre-earnings
» Post-earnings

The trading strategies used in these two scenarios are different and will be discussed in the sections that follow.

Pre-earnings

Trading a stock through a known coming event such as an earnings report comes with some inherent risk. You are essentially speculating on the contents of the news a company is going to release, and then more importantly, how investors and traders are going to interpret and react to that news release.

Even if you were privy to inside information about a company's financial results, it is possible that a CEO may comment that the outlook for the next quarter does not look that good. Forward-looking guidance almost always trumps past financial results. In this situation, the share price would react negatively to that news and drop despite the good earnings numbers. If you had bet for a move higher solely on the numbers, your trade would likely have been a loser.

Securities that have seen a significant price increase for weeks or even months before an earnings release are also at risk of the "buy the rumor, sell the news" phenomenon. Good news could already be priced in to the stock value, and once the results are released, investors and traders rush to take profits which can drive the stock price lower after the news event.

For example, Figure 15.1 shows a chart of Abnb Inc (ABNB), up to and after its earnings report. After the market closed on August 3rd, 2023, ABNB reported very strong earnings results which beat most of the analyst's expectations. Other metrics were also better than expected such as year over year increases in bookings. Given those results, many would have expected the ABNB share price to return to the recent high. But instead, traders hit the sell button and the stock price dropped despite strength in the travel sector overall.

Figure 15.1 Chart of ABNB showing reaction to the share price after a good earnings release (chart courtesy of Stockcharts.com).

Earnings Plays

The bottom line is that reactions to earnings releases or other known coming events can be unpredictable, and therefore one of the best ways to play these events is through the use of options. With options you can define your risk, or in other words, use a trade strategy where you know the maximum amount you will lose if you are wrong. Let's look at the Netflix, Inc (NFLX) earnings release as an example in Figure 15.2.

Figure 15.2 Chart of NFLX showing reaction to the share price after a good earnings release but weak forward-looking guidance (chart courtesy of Stockcharts.com).

Assume you were a trader that held a very bullish view on NFLX going into their earnings report on July 19, 2023. You see from the chart that there was a frenzy of buying just prior to the earnings date showing that you were not alone. However, after the CEO made some comments about weakening growth expectations looking forward, the stock price dropped significantly. If you had bought 100 shares of NFLX going into the earnings event, you could have been down $30.00 to $40.00 dollars per share which would have resulted in a loss of thousands of dollars.

Alternatively, with the same bullish view you could have used a bull call spread that we discussed in chapter 10. For example, you could have bought a $480.00 call and then sold a $500.00 call; both expiring at the end of the week on July 21st, which was after the earnings release. The cost of buying the ATM call and selling the OTM call would have resulted in a total investment of about $600.00, which is the maximum loss that would have been realized on a bad report. This loss was not a great outcome, but much better than losing thousands of dollars.

This highlights the advantage of using options to play an event with an unknown outcome. Of course, this is not the only options trade strategy you could have used in this situation. We have already discussed many options structures that could be used to make a bet on an earnings report. I have summarized some of the more popular options structures and the associated expected outcomes that the active trader hopes for in Table 15.1.

In summary, I rarely make swing trades before an earnings report or other event due to the unpredictable nature of the reaction after the news is released. However, there are many traders that are successful with these trades by getting big wins when they are right on the trade, and limiting their losses when they are wrong. It will be up to you to decide if this type of trade strategy is right for you.

Earnings Plays

Your Expected Price Reaction After News Release	Strategy Used	Risk	Reward
Little price change	Sell an ATM or OTM put and/or call	Potential for a large loss if the price changes a lot	Keep the premium collected from the sale
Little price change	Sell a vertical spread ATM or OTM put and/or call	Losses are capped if the price change is unexpectedly large	Keep the premium but it will be less because of the added options purchases
Large price move up or down (agnostic to direction)	Straddle - buy put and call ATM	Loss on investment if there is no big price move	Large price move sees one option price go up more that the loss seen with the other
Large price move up or down (agnostic to direction)	Strangle (buy a put and call OTM)	Loss on investment if there is no big price move	Large price move sees one option price go up more that the loss seen with the other
Large change up	Buy an OTM call	Loss on investment if security does not move up a lot	Potential for large profit on big move up
Large change up	Vertical call spread	Loss on investment if security does not move up a lot	Potential for large profit on big move up
Large change down	Buy OTM put	Loss on investment if security does not move down a lot	Potential for large profit on big move down
Large change down	Vertical put spread	Loss on investment if security does not move down a lot	Potential for large profit on big move down

Table 15.1 Table showing some popular options trade structures that could be used to hopefully profit from an earnings release.

125

Post-earnings

Trading options just after a news release is another way to take advantage of elevated volatility that often lingers after the event has taken place. This is my preferred way to use options, particularly after an earnings release or other company value changing events.

Veterans of Wall Street often talk about the 3-day rule, which refers to the period of time you should wait after a significant event happens to a company before taking a position. This is because it often takes a couple of days for a new share price to be established by market participants, given the recent news. Often momentum traders get involved during this period and drive the price to extremes either to the downside or upside. The trading opportunity often happens when the buying or selling frenzy begins to subside.

Figure 15.3 shows a chart of Amazon.com, Inc. (AMZN) after an earnings release on August 3rd, 2023. You can see from the chart, AMZN released a good earnings report and the share price responded accordingly by gapping up from the previous day's close. However, it could not hold the highs and ended up closing the day lower compared to where it opened. The next day it tried to rally again, but failed to make a new high while the volume dropped off significantly. Excitement about the earnings was already waning.

As an observant options trader with a trade plan to take positions after earnings, this AMZN earnings report offered a good opportunity for a short call options strategy, given a temporary top had been established by the momentum traders. In this case you could have shorted (sold) the $143.00 weekly calls and collected $1.40 or $140.00 per contract from the buyer. The bet was that AMZN would not go above $143.00 before the expiry of the weekly options. As it turned out, this trade worked as planned and you could have let them expire and keep the premium collected.

Earnings Plays

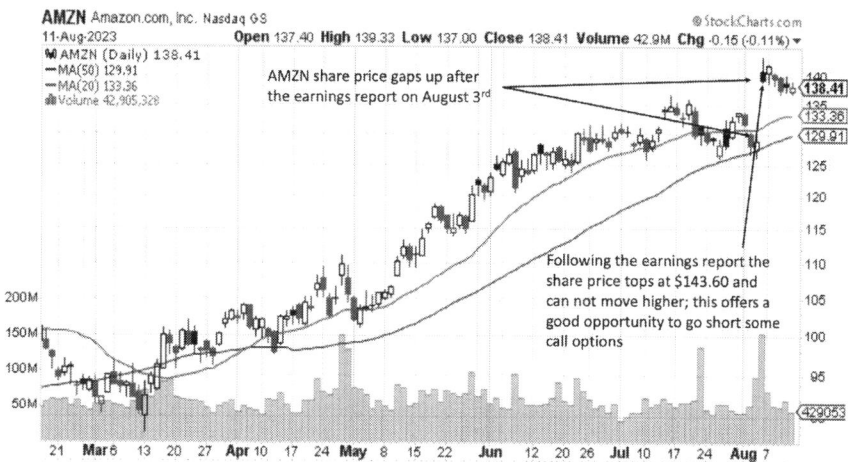

Figure 15.3 Chart of AMZN showing the price gap up after the earnings report but then unable to move higher after the event (chart courtesy of Stockcharts.com).

Another example of a news related event move occurred when Penn Entertainment Inc. (PENN) announced a $2 billion dollar deal with ESPN on August 8th, 2023. The news sent PENN stock flying higher, however there was an opposite reaction for one of PENN's main competitors, DraftKings Inc. (DKNG). DKNG price dropped significantly after the announcement as investors and traders saw the company losing business because of the PENN deal.

You can observe the chart of DKNG and the reaction to the news in Figure 15.4. This over-reaction to the deal represented an opportunity to take a long position with options. On the third day, as DKNG rallied back up with a low of around $27.50 per share, you could have sold some puts with that strike price expiring on that day for about $0.55 or $55.00 per contract. The stock finished strong into the close, and the puts expired worthless, so you would have kept the premium the buyer had paid for those puts.

Figure 15.4 Chart of DKNG after a negative reaction to a competitor deal. The over-reaction to the deal provided an opportunity to profit on the bounce back (chart courtesy of Stockcharts.com).

You might well ask, why not buy a call instead of selling the put? There are two reasons for using this selling strategy. The first reason was based on the belief that DKNG had finally bottomed in price on reaction to the news. There was no assurance that it the price would continue to go up during the day, but at very least, a trader using this strategy would have had a strong conviction that it had finished going down.

    Secondly, the cost of buying a call option would have included some premium (extrinsic value). Therefore, if a trader had bought an ATM call, the DKNG price would have needed to continue to go higher. The trade would not have been profitable until the stock price exceed the additional amount paid for the call option. Therefore, shorting the put had a higher probability of success, and because the price continued to go up after shorting the put, the trade was immediately in a profitable position.

    Remember that there are several ways to execute options trades. The strategies you use depend on the risk you are willing to take, the level of confidence that you have for the trade, your ability to manage the risk, and overall market conditions. As we have already discussed, vertical spreads are a good way to manage your risk by defining the maximum loss you can incur on a trade.

Many traders are reluctant to hold risky swing positions overnight or for several days to weeks, because they feel they are exposed to news events that can happen when the market is closed. This is another reason I like to trade options after earnings, because a company is unlikely to come out with any additional news after an earnings release. If they had announced bad or good news during the earnings call, they are very unlikely to come out with another significant release one week later.

That is not to say that some news couldn't come out soon after a release, such as an SEC investigation into the company. This is why you need to consider added risk management strategies such as taking reasonable sized trades.

In Table 15.2 I have summarized a few of the options trade strategies discussed above that can be used to take a position, and possibly profit, after the reaction to a news event has taken place.

In summary, I prefer trading options after earnings as opposed to before earnings. This is only my personal preference, and you may find that it is much more profitable to make trade decisions going into earnings for a bigger win. For the purpose of this introductory book, I have chosen to discuss some of the more basic options strategies that can be used to trade earnings releases or other known major news events. There are many other strategies that can be used such as using options with different expiry dates. As you get more familiar with trading options you may want to investigate these more complicated approaches.

Your Expected Price Move Several Days after a News Release	Strategy Used	Risk	Reward
Little price change after a big move in either direction	Sell a put and/or call	Potential for a large loss if the price changes a lot	Keep the premium collected from the sale
Little price change after a big move in either direction	Sell vertical call spread and/or vertical put spread	Potential for loss but they are capped if the price changes a lot	Keep the premium but it will be less because of the added option purchases
Price drop, bottoming and then a reversal in trend back up after a sell off	Buy a call close to ITM	If a significant trend reversal does not happen – call expires worthless	Profits will be good if there is a large price reversal back up
Price drop, bottoming and then a reversal in trend back up after a sell off	Sell an OTM put at or just below the established low	If bottom has not been established then you could see a significant loss on the position	Put expires worthless and you keep the premium from sale of put
Price drop, bottoming and then a reversal trend back up after a sell off	Use a bullish vertical call spread	If a bottom has not been established then there are smaller losses due to lower cost of trade	Profit capped with the vertical call spread due to sale of OTM call
Price rise, topping and then a reversal trend back down after a buying spree	Buy a put close to ITM	If a significant trend reversal does not happen – put expires worthless	Profits will be good if there is a large price reversal back down
Price rise, topping and then a reversal in trend back down after a buying spree	Sell an OTM call at or just above the established high	If top has not been established then you could see a significant loss on the position	Call expires worthless and you keep the premium from sale of put
Price rise, topping and then a reversal in trend back down after a buying spree	Use a bearish vertical put spread	If a top has not been established then there are smaller losses due to lower cost of trade	Profit capped with the vertical put spread due to sale of OTM put

Table 15.2 A table that summarizes a number of ways you can trade a news release after a period of time has passed and any over-reaction starts to subside.

Earnings Plays

CHAPTER SUMMARY

Options are a very good instrument to use to make profitable trades in and around company events such as, but not limited to, earnings releases. This chapter is summarized below:

- » Earnings releases and other expected news release events represent a very good opportunity to use options to make a profit.
- » Options can be used to realize profits by placing a trade either before the news release or after the news release has occurred.
- » Trading a stock through a known coming event such as an earnings report comes with some inherent risk due to the unknown outcome.
- » Using options allows the trader to make a bet on an outcome without unlimited risk. Options allow you to define the most that you can lose on a trade if you are wrong.
- » A trader can set up their options positions depending on whether they are betting on a big move up in price, a big move down, or a result where the price moves very little after the release.
- » Depending on the expected reaction after the news release, a number of different trade setups were presented in a table.
- » Another strategy to trade news releases involves waiting until the news is released and set up your options positions after the new price of the security is established.
- » Waiting until after the release eliminates a lot of the unknown that a trader must deal with before the news event.
- » Once new highs or lows are established after a news event, a trader can take a position with some confidence that, in the immediate future, no additional news that could move the price of the security a lot will be forthcoming.
- » A table was provided that summarized the possible reactions of a stock after a news release and trade positions that could be taken for a profit based on the expected reaction.

131

CHAPTER 16

Day Trading Using Options

As I have mentioned previously, options can be used in any type of trading be it day trading, swing trading, or by a long-term investor. In this chapter I will focus on the opportunity to profitably day trade options. The scope of this book is not to teach you how to day trade, but I will show you how powerful options can be when used with this type of trading.

No aspiring options trader should attempt to day trade using options until they have mastered day trading in stocks. There are several reasons for this which I will discuss below:

- » Building Experience and a Trade Book
- » Leverage
- » Complexity of Options

Building Experience and a Trade Book

The first thing I want to emphasize is that day trading is not a profession you can jump into and get rich quickly. There is no shortage of bloggers and online imposters who want you to believe otherwise. They say that all you need to do is follow their simple process of "buy low, sell high" or "buy the dip, sell the rally". Day trading can be made to look deceptively easy, but it is not.

However, if you are willing to put in the effort to learn this trade, day trading can be a profitable profession. It takes practice and experience to become a consistently profitable trader. That is why our community at Bearbulltraders.com (BBT) spends so much time and effort on educating and mentoring our members. The founder of BBT, Andrew Aziz has written one of the best books available on the topic of day trading called "How to Day Trade for a Living". I suggest you check his book out if you have not already.

The education provided at BBT includes what to look for on charts and graphs for good entries and exits on trades including, but not limited to the following:

- » previous day high and low price
- » previous day closing price
- » volume weighted average price (VWAP) level
- » moving averages
- » reading the time and sales tape
- » chart patterns such as double bottoms, ABCD, double tops, head and shoulders
- » reading the level 2
- » break outs on a high price of the day
- » break downs on a low price of the day
- » multiple time frame break outs or break downs

Part of the BBT educational process revolves around helping a new trader find their edge, or in other words, find out what kind of trades they prefer to use. This is often based on personality and risk tolerance.

Everyone is different, so a type of trade that works for one person may not be suitable for another. This is why a trader will develop their own personal trade book which is a plan that details what type of trades they will take, under what conditions, where they will enter, and where they will exit (either getting stopped out for a small loss or taking profits).

Once you have your trade book developed, and you have practiced a lot in a simulator, you are ready for trading with real money which can present another challenge. This is where emotions start to play a significant role in your decision-making and will test you on whether you can stick to your trade book plan. At BBT we spend a lot of time discussing the mental aspect of trading.

Our brain has developed in a way that makes most of us bad traders. Our genetically programed fear of pain and loss cause us to hold on to losing trades too long because we are reluctant to feel the pain of a realized loss. It also causes us to sell our winners too soon because we fear we may lose what we have gained.

For these reasons, it is in your best interest to learn the art of day trading by simply buying and selling stocks. Mastering stock trading, and having a good trade book you can rely on for profitable returns, will allow you to execute the more complicated options trades with confidence.

Leverage

Leverage essentially allows you to use your capital in a way that gets you a better return. In chapter 5, I discussed how trading options on a stock can offer you a much higher percentage return on your money invested compared to trading the shares of that same stock.

As another example, let's look at a 5-minute chart of NVDA shown in Figure 16.1 that covers the entire trading day of August 15th, 2023. You can see that NVDA opened at a high of day around $451.00, and immediately sold off to make what turned out to be the low of the trading day, at the previous day's closing price of about $437.00. The shares price action created a common pattern called a "double bottom" at this level and then reversed to go back up.

How to Trade Options

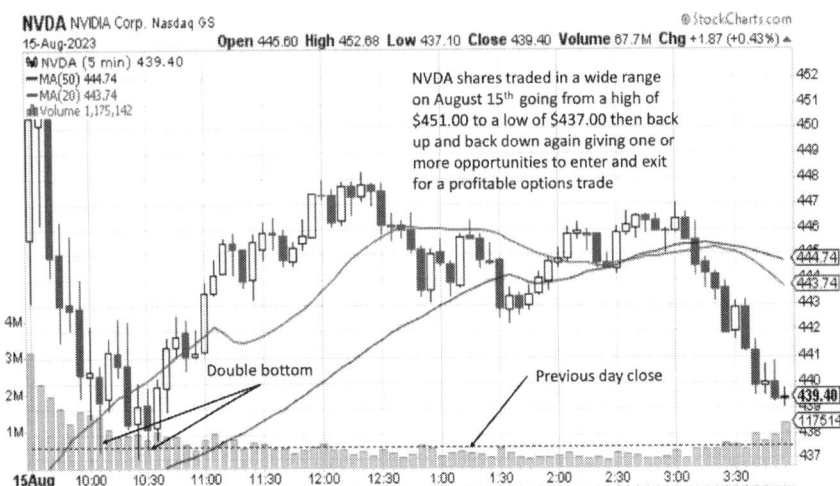

Figure 16.1 Chart of NVDA with 5-minute candles covering the entire trading day's price moves from a high of $451 to a low of $437.00 (chart courtesy of Stockcharts.com).

Several opportunities presented themselves for day traders on this day. Support for a share price often occurs at the previous day's closing price. This is almost exactly where the NVDA share price reversed. The double bottom was another confirmation that a price reversal was more than likely going to occur around the $437.00 level.

As a day trader, let's assume you would have seen this setup and bought 100 shares of NVDA for about $439.00 per share for a cost of $43,900.00. As an options trader, you could have bought one NVDA $440.00 weekly option representing 100 shares for a price of about $9.50. For this option trade you would have chosen to use a close to ITM weekly option because it would have a relatively high delta. Recall that the high delta means the stock and option price move up or down close to the same dollar amount.

As the NVDA share price went back up to $447.00 on the bounce from previous day close, you would have seen a respectable $8.00 per share move on the price. The 100-share purchase resulted in a $800.00 gain which is a 2% return on the $43,900.00 investment.

In comparison, the option you purchased at $9.50 could have been sold for a price of $13.50 which is a $400.00 gain on a $900.00 investment. That is more than a 40% return on your $900.00 investment which is a lot better than 2%.

The NVDA example illustrates how using options can give you a much greater return on investment, but can also lead to a much higher percentage loss if you have misjudged the trade setup. This is why you need to be proficient in day trading, and have a trading plan, so you know where to stop out and take a small loss on your trade if it does not go in your favor.

Complexity of Options

As you are likely aware, trading options is a little more complicated compared to going long or short stocks. You have additional choices to make when trading options, including strike price and expiry date. For this reason, it is most likely in your best interest to learn to day trade stocks before switching over to options.

Once you have a trade book developed with your trading plans in place, you can start to refine your plan to include options. You have to consider that placing an options trade can take a few seconds longer. It is not as simple as hitting a hot key or button to buy or sell a stock. You have to go through a process of selecting your expiry date, and choosing an appropriate strike price, before hitting the buy or sell key.

Whatever underlying security you are considering for a trade, you want to be sure that the options are actively traded. This usually ensures that the difference between the bid and the ask (the spread) is close together. Trading options with very wide spreads means that it is often difficult to get a good entry price. Exiting a trade can also be more difficult and costly if the spread is wide. This large difference will eat into your profits, or if you need to stop out, increase your losses.

In summary, trading options is a little more complex compared to trading securities, but easily learned by most traders with a little

How to Trade Options

education and practice. Once mastered, you will have an opportunity to make much more profitable trades (on a return-on-investment basis) while using a lot less capital.

CHAPTER SUMMARY

The following is a summary of this chapter where I discussed the opportunity to use options for day trading:

- » No aspiring options trader should attempt to day trade using options until they have mastered day trading in stocks.
- » Day trading is not a profession you can jump into and get rich quickly. It can be made to look deceptively easy, but it is not.
- » This book is not written to teach you how to day trade. Andrew Aziz has written one of the best books available on the topic of day trading called "How to Day Trade for a Living".
- » The BBT community offers a complete and extensive set of educational videos, webinars and books on day trading. The education revolves around helping a new trader find their edge and manage their emotions.
- » There are many day trading setups and it is important for an aspiring day trader to determine which ones will work best for them and their personality.
- » Using options can give you a much greater return on investment, but can also lead to a much higher percentage loss if you have misjudged the trade setup. This is why you need to be proficient in day trading, and have a trading plan so you know where to stop out and take a small loss on your trade if it does not go in your favor.

» Trading options is a little more complicated compared to going long or selling short stocks. You have additional choices to make when trading options which include strike price and expiry date. For this reason, it is most likely in your best interest to learn to day trade stocks before switching over to options.

CHAPTER 17
Unusual Options Activity

Unusual options activity refers to a security whose options are experiencing an abnormal level of buying or selling. An options trading volume of 5 times the daily average is considered to be "unusual" based on a rule of thumb that has been adopted by most traders.

For example, consider an ITM call option on Applied Materials Inc. (AMAT) that trades about 200 contracts per day, assuming there is no event news that has just occurred or is pending. If there was a sudden surge in volume where the same options traded over 1,000 contracts in a day, you would consider that suspicious, and possibly worthy of further investigation.

It is important to understand that a surge in options volume activity does not necessarily translate into a bullish or bearish indicator that should be acted on. From reading this book, you should now know that there are a number of reasons options are traded. A pick up in options activity could be a large investor hedging, or in other words, taking insurance out on a current portfolio position.

The unusual options activity in underlying securities can happen for several reasons:

» A single large fund or institution entering or exiting a position for any number of reasons related to their portfolio of securities.

» Options traders speculating on upcoming news such as an earnings release, essentially making bets on the outcome and security's price reaction.

- » Rumors of a possible merger or acquisition which still falls under the category of speculation, but in this case, there is no "official" pending news.
- » While it is illegal, on rare occasions unusual options trades can be the result of insiders or others with non-public company information taking positions in advance of a value changing event.

Let's look at an interesting example of unusual options activity that occurred on the stock of Splunk Inc. (SPLK). On September 20th, 2023 SPLK stock was trading at a price of about $120.00 per share. The following morning Cisco Systems, Inc. (CSCO) announced they were making an all-cash offer to buy SPLK. This caused SPLK price to rocket higher to $145.00 per share as shown in Figure 17.1.

Figure 17.1 Chart of SPLK leading up to the CSCO buy-out announcement and corresponding rise in price
(chart courtesy of Stockcharts.com).

Of course, buy-outs happen all the time. However, the day before the buy-out announcement, there was an alleged $22,000 purchase of SPLK $127.00 strike calls that were expiring on September 22nd, 2023. The buyer paid a minimal amount of $0.04 for each call because the calls were so far OTM and expiring in 2 days. By all measures this would have been considered a real "you only live once" (YOLO) trade, purchasing $22,000.00 worth of options that had an almost zero chance of paying off unless some major event occurred. Apparently, this worked out for a lucky trader who turned the $22,000.00 investment into $10 million.

Regardless, you do need to be cautious when reading into unusual options trade activity. Remember that every option trade has a buyer and a seller. You might be drawn into thinking that a large volume of call options activity is a bullish sign because calls are associated with prices moving up. But you need to consider that the large call options activity you are seeing could be a fund, with a sizable holding of the underlying security, looking to generate additional yield by selling covered calls. This was discussed in chapter 11.

The same reasoning would hold for unusual put options activity. Seeing put activity, you may initially think that this is a bearish sign for the underlying security. However, referring back to chapter 9, traders can take a bullish trade on a stock by selling ITM puts with the hope that the underlying security stays around where it is, or moves up in price. Then at a later date, they can buy the puts back at a lower price, or let them expire worthless and keep the money received from the put sale.

Regardless of the reason for the increased volume, an options trader can use this information to find potential trading and profit opportunities. There are some brokers that offer options scanners to their customers for free on their trading platforms. There are also online options services that offer more advanced scanners which can filter out the many small trades that are placed by retail traders, versus the single large trades that are placed by the larger institutions and big investors. Subscribers to these platforms usually pay a monthly or annual fee.

There are 2 types of unusual options activity, conducted by larger players, where you should focus your attention when scanning for opportunities. They are summarized as follows.

1. **Block trades:** A block trade occurs when a large number of options are bought or sold at a specific price. The number of contracts is often in the thousands but it is also important to look at the value the trader is committing to the trade. Block trades are usually done by institutional investors.

2. **Sweep trades:** Sweep trades are a group of smaller trades executed on the same underlying security, done at or near the same time, and across a number of exchanges. These types of options trades could be an institution attempting to hide the position they are taking by breaking a large trade into smaller orders.

In the past, options traders were mostly institutions, and therefore considered to be the "smart money" crowd because trading in options was considered a little more complex compared to buying and selling stocks. This perception has changed since 2020.

There has been a big uptick in options activity caused by retail traders jumping into the so called meme stocks, and participating in "swarm trading", where retail traders pile into specific stocks and options. These retail traders saw and experienced the power of options leverage, some making huge returns, and many seeing their accounts wiped out.

Regardless, with a good options scanner, unusual options activity is a good starting point for traders to look for opportunities. Starting with a scan to identify unusual activity, you can do more due diligence on the security to see if there is a case you can build for opening a position. The steps in the due diligence process could be the following:

» Scanners can look for a number of different criteria such as high-volume block trades, big changes in open interest on a contract price, specific options combinations (vertical spreads), or large price changes at a specific price or expiry date. You will need to decide on what metric you want to focus your scan.

» Identify the strike prices and expiry dates that are flagged by the scanner. Is there something important about those dates or prices?

» Try to identify the catalyst for the unusual activity. Is there a news event coming up soon such as an earnings release or the outcome of a trial being done by a drug company? Coming news events can often lead traders to speculate on the outcome.

» If there is an obvious catalyst, you can decide if you want to take a position as well by looking at market conditions, fundamentals of the underlying asset, and some technical analysis.

» With no obvious catalyst you can do the same analysis described above, with the understanding that institutions take large positions in options contracts for many reasons, other than speculation on a big move as we already discussed in this chapter.

Following your due diligence, you may decide to take an options position based on what you have learned. As with all trades, you must create and follow a trade plan that would include the entry strike price, expiry date, where you will take profits, and at what price you will stop out of the trade if it does not work out as hoped.

In conclusion, scanning for unusual options activity can be a good place for an options trader to start when searching for trading opportunities. But you do need to exercise caution because there are many reasons large trades occur, and it is your job to figure out why and whether it is worth your investment dollars.

CHAPTER SUMMARY

In this chapter, I discussed unusual options activity which happens regularly in the market as summarized below:

- » Unusual options activity refers to a security whose options are experiencing an abnormal level of buying or selling.
- » An options trading volume of 5 times the daily average is considered to be unusual based on a rule of thumb.
- » A surge in options activity does not necessarily translate into a bullish or bearish indicator. There are many reasons that this activity can occur.
- » Reasons for unusual activity can include institutions trading for their portfolios, buying or selling based on a known news event pending, rumors circulating about a specific company, or even illegal insider trading.
- » There are scanners available to look for this activity. Some brokers offer a scanner as part of their platform. There is web based paid services that offer sophisticated scanning services as well.
- » It is often better to watch how institutional traders are taking positions. Their activity can show up as "block trades" (large single trades) or as "sweep trades" which are multiple small trades all taken at the same time across a number of platforms.
- » Unusual options activity is a good starting point for traders to look for opportunities.
- » Similar to all types of trades you take, you should start with due diligence to find a possible reason for the abnormal trade activity.
- » If you decide that the activity is providing a trade opportunity, you should create and follow a trading plan which includes entry strike price, expiry date, where you will take profits, and at what price you will stop out.

CHAPTER 18

Maximum Pain

As traders and investors, we have all experienced the pain of having to exit a losing trade and taking a loss. If you trade options, you will experience that pain as well, but what about max pain? Fortunately, it is not what you might think the title of this chapter implies.

Max pain or the max pain price, is the strike price where the most options holders will experience financial loss on expiry. This idea comes from the belief that most of the options traders that hold their long positions until expiry will lose their investment. Statistical analysis shows us that about 60% of options are traded out before expiry, 30% expire worthless, and about 10% of options get exercised. Or in other words, the options holder ends up with the shares of the underlying security.

So how can this information about max pain price help you with your options trades? The max pain belief comes from the idea that a security will move toward this max pain strike price as we close in on the expiry date. The reason this happens is because a lot of the options transactions are done by market makers. Market makers do not want to take on huge risks so they hedge their positions. As an example, if a market maker sold 10 OTM call options contracts on AAPL, they may buy 1000 shares of AAPL as a hedge, in case AAPL moved above the strike price before expiry.

This is the balancing act that the market makers play all day. Buying and selling securities and options while making sure that they are not exposed to big unexpected moves that could result in them taking a huge loss.

As the options expiry date approaches, it is now in the market maker's financial interest to drive the stock price to a level that is going to cause as many options as possible to expire worthless. Those market makers that have sold a lot of calls want to drive the price of the underlying security down. Conversely, those that have written a lot of puts want to see the price go higher, so the options expire worthless. This is where the idea of the max pain price comes from.

The max pain theory is not without its detractors, and many believe that security prices will naturally move to an area of the most pain regardless, and it is not a case of some possible manipulation.

When it comes to determining the max pain price, fortunately there are some web services that will do that cumbersome calculation for you. The calculation involves summing up the dollar value of all the puts and calls that are ITM, for a strike price which is not practical to do for an options trader. Depending on how actively traded the options on a particular security, max pain price can change hour by hour as the expiry time draws to close which is why a service that does this calculation is invaluable.

In closing the discussion on the max pain theory, it is possible that large market players will try to influence the closing price of a security on an expiry day. This is why you might see an odd surge or drop in a security's price just before the close of the trading day. If the price is close to the max pain price, then you could see the price move there as the trading day ends. If it is far away from the max pain price, it might move that direction even though the price does not close there.

CHAPTER SUMMARY

In this chapter i covered the theory of max pain price. Important points in the chapter include the following:

- » Max pain or the max pain price, is the strike price where the most options holders will experience financial loss on expiry.
- » This idea is based on the belief that most of the options traders that hold their long positions until expiry will lose their investment.
- » It is in the market maker's financial interest to drive the stock price to a level that is going to cause as many options as possible to expire worthless. This situation nets them the most money on all the options that they have sold.
- » When it comes to determining the max pain price, there are some web services that will do that cumbersome calculation for you.
- » On options expiry days, you might see an odd surge or drop in a security's price just before the end of the trading day. These could be large market players using their buying and selling power to move the closing price to an area of max pain.

CHAPTER 19
Triple Witching

This chapter will deal with an event referred to as triple witching. This event happens when monthly stock options, stock index options, and stock index futures expire on the same trading day. It happens four times a year on the third Friday of March, June, September, and December. On these specific days, you may see some unusual price movements and added trading volume.

One of the reasons you may see some added trading volume and volatility is because some of the options and futures holders may allow their contracts to expire, which then requires a purchase or sale of the underlying security. These purchases and sales add to volume and price action in both the underlying asset and the derivatives (options and futures).

Added volume may also be caused by options and futures holders that do not want to stay in their positions into expiration. They either close their positions or close their positions and open new ones. This is referred to as "rolling out". This unusual volume and price action is particularly noticeable in the final hour of the trading day.

The final hours of triple witching can draw in arbitrageurs who are looking for small market inefficiencies caused by the increased buying, selling and settling of positions. The small price imbalances can represent profit opportunities for them which creates additional trading volume, but does not offer the retail trader any potential trades.

Triple witching is an event that options traders should be aware of and acknowledge on these four days of the year where there could be some abnormal price action and volume. Apart from that, these trading days do not offer any potential for a retail trader to make a profit.

CHAPTER SUMMARY

In this chapter I discussed an event that is relevant to options traders, referred to as triple witching. Important points in the chapter include the following:

- » Triple witching happens when monthly stock options, stock index options, and stock index futures expire on the same trading day.
- » It happens four times a year on the third Friday of March, June, September, and December.
- » On these four specific days there may be some unusual price movements and added trading volume.
- » Added volume happens because some of the options and futures holders may allow their contracts to expire which then requires the purchase or sale of the underlying security.
- » Holders of derivatives may be closing positions and possibly adding new ones which is sometimes referred to as "rolling out".
- » These trading days generally do not offer any potential for a retail trader to make a profitable trade, but they should be aware of when it is happening and what to expect on that day.

CHAPTER 20
Risk Management

Whether you are trading stocks or options, for me, risk management is one of the most important aspects of trading and managing money. I covered this topic in my previous books but it is worth reviewing and reinforcing. Preserving your capital is the most crucial thing you can do as a trader or investor.

As a trader, the money you are investing in the market, your capital, is one of your most important and vital tools. Without capital there is no way for you to make money, no matter how many other tools and skills you might possess. Protecting your capital should, therefore, be your highest priority. In order to successfully do just that, there are four essential processes you must perform:

» Assessing risk and the reward
» Setting stops and targets
» Manage trade size
» Diversify your holdings

Let's look at these four important risk and account management processes in more detail in the following sections.

Assessing Risk and Reward

Your most important objective in any type of trading is to manage your risk. Your goal should not be to buy and sell options – it is to make a profit. Because of commissions, your broker is the only guaranteed winner when you are buying and selling options in the market. Your job is to manage your risk and your account. Whenever you click buy or sell on your option trading platform, you expose your money to a risk of loss.

An unsuccessful trader will likely look at an entry and only think about how much they are going to make on a trade. A successful trader will always consider what is the upside and the downside on any particular trade. In other words, you should ask yourself how much you are risking if you have to take a loss. This has nothing to do with being right or wrong on a trade. It is about comparing the risk you are taking to the reward you hope to get from the trade. If you are risking a loss of $100.00 on a trade and only expect to get $50.00 as the upside reward, then this is NOT a good risk-to-reward ratio.

To have a viable trade setup, you should expect to get at least 2 times the reward in comparison to the risk that you are taking. Obviously, the possibility of having more than 2 times the reward is even better. If you use this risk-to-reward strategy in your trading, you will still be marginally profitable even if you are wrong on all of your trades 60% of the time.

In my previous books I discussed, in depth, how to recognize good trading setups and then determine advantageous entry and exit prices. This then enables you to calculate the risk-to-reward of each trade you are considering entering. A good trade setup will always offer you 2 times or more reward for the risk that you are taking.

Setting Stops and Targets

Now that I have discussed the concept of risk-to-reward, the next step is to understand how to put this into action. A stop-loss is a must for a successful trader, and it is one of the most important tools you will use to preserve your capital. A winning trader must believe that their stop-loss is one of their best friends. Any trading system or strategy will have losses – that is a given. A successful trader accepts a loss and moves on from their losing trade.

Once you have conducted a complete assessment of a trade, and determined that your potential reward is at least (if not better than) 2 times your risk, you will push the buy or sell button. Your capital is now at risk and you need to set your stop-loss price. This stop point is the price level you have determined in advance, will be where you will exit the trade if it does not go in the direction you are anticipating. You need to trade your plan, and if necessary, get out of your position before a small loss becomes a big loss.

It may sound simple enough to faithfully commit to making a trading plan and then subsequently following that plan, but novice traders (and veterans too!) can get caught up in the emotion of the trade. They start reading all of the online hype and begin to daydream about what they are going to buy with their profits.

They don't consider the possibility of the trade not working out, and will not allow themselves to take a loss because it seems like an admission of failure. Rather than taking a small loss and moving on, they reassess and rationalize why they believe the trade will eventually turn in their favor.

Remember these words of wisdom from the famous economist John Maynard Keynes:

> "The market can remain irrational longer than you can remain solvent."

The discipline in following your trading plan also applies to taking profits at your expected target price. When a trade becomes a winner, you will be inclined to immediately take a profit to reinforce your inherent need to be right. Some traders want to believe that they can achieve a high win/loss ratio, and as long as they close out a trade profitably, they will then be a profitable trader. A novice trader may see a profit in a trade, but instead of sticking with their planned exit strategy, they will take profits before their target is hit, fearing that their gain will reverse and turn into a loss.

Unfortunately, taking profits too early negates the process you initially went through to determine your risk-to-reward ratio. By exiting a trade early, you may be barely getting a 1 to 1 risk-to-reward ratio. That means you now need to be right 50% of the time merely to break-even. Those odds are not nearly as good as getting at least 2 times the reward in comparison to the risk you are taking. You surely do not want to spend all of that time and effort just to break-even.

There are, nonetheless, occasions when you will want to change your original trading plan. If you are a longer-term trader, you have the luxury of time, and therefore the ability to monitor your existing positions and trades as they unfold. This does not mean that you should be continually making changes to your trading plan because of every little gyration in a particular position. However, on a very regular basis you should confirm that nothing significant has fundamentally changed. If something of consequence has changed, you will want to reconsider your stops and target exit prices.

The ability to manage your options trades usually comes down to controlling your emotions, and that is definitely easier said than done.

Managing Trade Size

Managing and controlling how much capital you invest in one trade is another very important component of trading. Even with the best planning and strategies, you will never know at the time you enter a trade whether it will become a winner or if it will turn into a loser. Accordingly, you should not overcommit your capital to any one options trade.

Most experienced traders use the rule of thumb that says you should not put more than 2% of your capital at risk on any one trade. This means that if you have $20,000.00 of capital in your account, you should not put more than $400.00 at risk on a trade (2% of $20,000.00). Let's take a look at how this would apply to an imaginary trade.

Assume you are looking at an option that is trading at $2.00 per contract which represents a $200.00 purchase (plus commission). The price movements of the underlying security suggest that its price will go higher from its current price of $10.00 to $11.00 where you expect it will find some price resistance. You like this trade because you can see price support of the underlying security at around $9.75 (where a low had been made on some bottoming price action). So, if you get an entry price of about $2.00 per contract, and the delta is 0.70, you can expect that the option will trade up to a new value of $2.70 if the trade works out as hoped with the one dollar move higher.

If the underlying stock price drops to your stop out price of $9.75, the contract you purchased would now be worth about $1.80 based on the 0.70 delta (a $0.25 move lower with a 0.70 delta equals about a $0.20 move lower for the options price). This is a good trade because the reward is more than 3 times the risk (reward $0.70 versus $0.20 risk). Do not forget what I mentioned earlier. You should always expect to get 2 times or more reward for any risk you take.

The question then arises, "How much should I buy?" In other words, "What is the most money that I should put into this trade?" Using the previous example of an account with $20,000.00 total capital, you should be risking no more than $400.00. With a stop-loss of $0.20 per contract below your entry at $2.00, you would purchase no more than 20 contracts ($400.00 divided by $0.20 per contract). Therefore, if you do get stopped out, you will lose about $400.00 based on holding 20 contracts.

Of course, a loss of any kind is not what you are hoping for. But by limiting your investment, you also limit your loss to 2% of your capital. By properly managing your stop-losses and the amount of money you put at risk in each trade, you will ensure that you survive to trade another day.

I realize that this approach flies in the face of the "You Only Live Once" (YOLO) trading style that you will see touted on sites like WallStreetBets. YOLO trades, which became quite popular in 2020, are more akin to gambling and have nothing in common with taking a thoughtful investment approach to trading.

To be clear, there are a considerable number of people who have made small and large fortunes using the YOLO philosophy. It is easy to find stories online about successful YOLO trades. Unfortunately, there are also people who have made a bet on a security that did not work out and in the process lost a significant amount of their savings. You are not apt to hear as much about those trades.

Traders who use the YOLO strategy need to be prepared for the possibility that they may suffer some deep losses. You need to take that potential for loss into account. Ask yourself, "Will a big loss cause financial hardship, family stress or depression?" If not, then maybe a roll of the dice with money you can afford to lose will work out. But you must recognize that this is certainly an unorthodox way to grow your wealth.

Diversifying Your Holdings

Diversification is a tool utilized by many financial advisors and investors to spread the allocation of capital over a broad range of financial instruments and sectors. One of the major risks an active trader or investor faces is waking up to find that some substantial and undesirable news has been released on a stock they are currently holding. This can be a devastating development if they have made a relatively large commitment to the particular stock.

Unfortunately, no one can predict these events and if you are a swing or position trader, you are constantly being exposed to this type of risk. Eventually you will be affected by it. Two ways that you can mitigate this risk are to invest or trade in ETFs, and to limit the size of any single stock you invest in.

One of the key advantages of trading ETF options is the portfolio diversification that these financial instruments offer. Since ETFs are composed of a group of holdings, if one of the holdings is impacted by some news, the other holdings may see little to no impact at all, therefore minimizing any overall losses in the ETF and their associated options.

However, some ETFs have a specific focus. It might be utilities, technology, industrials, a currency, or a stock index, to name a few. There can always be negative market news that will impact a whole sector, and that can cause the ETF to drop in value. But it will not likely drop as much as, for instance, the stock of a company undergoing an SEC investigation for possible fraud.

There are many options traders that just trade stock index ETFs such as the Invesco QQQ Trust (QQQ). These index ETFs are very liquid making them easy to trade in and out of without taking a big loss between the bid and ask prices. They have daily expiry dates making them well suited to those that focus on day trading.

In summary, you should monitor your individual stock investments and make certain that no single holding is a significant part of your portfolio. ETFs can provide a good level of risk management when it comes to individual stock news events. However, they can also be vulnerable to negative news that hits the entire sector that they are focused on.

CHAPTER SUMMARY

In chapter 20, I discussed how an investor or trader must protect one of the most important trading tools: their capital. There are a number of rules that you can follow to ensure that you do not have an issue with a significant loss of capital. Some of these rules and major points about risk management that I covered in this chapter are listed below:

- » Protect your capital: without it you cannot be an investor or trader.

- » Leave your ego at the door and submit to the market and price action. Remember, *"the market can remain irrational longer than you can remain solvent."*

- » Always assess the reward and the risk you are taking on a trade. A good trade is one where you get at least twice the reward versus the potential loss you may suffer if the trade does not go as planned.

- » Honor your stop-loss. Do not let small losses turn into big losses.

- » Respect your target price and do not take profits too early unless something significant has changed your outlook.

- » Learn and respect that having some losses is part of the trading game. Do not take it personally.

- » Constantly review your existing trades to ensure that nothing significant has changed. If something of fundamental consequence has changed, you will then want to reconsider your stops and target exit prices. This is the only reason you should consider changing your trading plan.

- » Actively manage the size of each trade so that you do not risk more than 2% of your capital.

CHAPTER 21
Journaling Your Trades

When it comes to industrial production, we often hear the phrase, "what gets measured gets improved". This is only partially true. For example, if you are growing a vegetable garden and want to ensure a good crop, you will want to regularly confirm that the garden is getting enough water. However, putting a rain gauge out and measuring the rainfall during your growing season is not going to be sufficient to guarantee you a bountiful crop of vegetables. While it is important to know how much rain your garden is receiving, it is equally important to have a plan in place to act on the information that you collect. In the case of your garden, you can measure the rainfall and if the plants are not getting adequate water, then you take action and water them.

It is the same for almost any system or process. You need to measure performance (very important), and use that information to determine what actions you can take to improve. This is one of the main reasons why keeping a trade journal is so integral to being a successful trader.

From a risk management perspective, the use of a trade journal provides you with a record of the trading plan you have diligently researched and put in place when you entered a trade. This record contains your entry price, the price you will stop out, and where you will take profits. Without a record of your trading plan, you may forget some of these important price levels. A documented plan may also help prevent you from making snap emotional decisions in the middle of a trade. These emotion-driven decisions often negate all the initial work you put into building a good trading plan.

There are many ways to maintain a trade journal, and the process you follow will be up to you and your personal preferences. Everyone is different, so you need to figure out what works best for your personality. Because your trades will unfold over days to months, it may be optimal to keep some sort of an electronic-based or paper-based recording system or log.

There are a number of web-based journaling platforms, including TraderSync, TradesViz and TradeZella. Each platform has a free subscription level which offers a limited number of tracking options. Fees then apply to unlock additional features. If you lean toward using a web-based platform for journaling activities, I suggest you research a number of these sites to decide if one of them will meet your needs.

Regardless of what system or platform you choose to use, the following are items I suggest you keep track of concerning each trade:

- » date
- » options details including strike price and expiry date chosen
- » entry price of options
- » stop out price
- » target price or prices
- » market internals: i.e., conditions overall, S&P, Nasdaq, industry sector
- » source of trade idea
- » reasoning for entering trade
- » sector alignment, "Is the trade you are considering aligned with the market and sector direction?"
- » technical indicators you may have used

- » pertinent upcoming events should you prefer to avoid holding through such events as earnings releases or drug trial result
- » a risk-to-reward ratio ≥ 2
- » actual exit price or prices
- » profit/loss
- » any and all comments you might have or whatever seems relevant to you at the time. This may include notes on the trade as well as on your execution and your level of confidence versus the actual trade result

In summary, a trade journal will solidify your trading plan by documenting where you entered each trade that you took. And most importantly, where you stopped out if the trade did not go as you had expected. This is critical in managing your capital and surviving to trade another day.

CHAPTER SUMMARY

In chapter 21, I discussed the importance of maintaining a trading journal. The following is a summary of the chapter:

- » As a trader or investor, you need to measure performance, and use that information to determine what actions you can take to improve.
- » Use of a trade journal provides you with a record of the trading plan you have diligently researched and created. This record helps you follow that plan and reduces the temptation to make random changes based on emotions that come up from moment to moment.
- » Maintain your trade journal and review it regularly to ensure you are documenting and following your plan for each options trade.
- » A journal allows you to assess the performance of your trade strategies and make changes or modifications as needed.

CHAPTER 22
Final Thoughts

In this book, I delved into what options are and how they work, some of the basic ways options trades can be structured, as well as outlining a number of strategies that you can employ to make profitable trades. You should now understand that options can be used to protect gains in existing stock positions, generate income, or simply be traded for profit as you would other kinds of securities.

In closing, I always feel the need to emphasize that managing your financial affairs requires effort and time. This is true no matter what type of trading you choose to pursue, be it day trading, swing trading, or position trading. Developing a consistent routine of checking in with the markets, scanning for potential opportunities, staying in touch with trends, and actively monitoring your positions is a process that you will need to regularly follow.

Regardless of whether you are actively trading options or stocks, always have a trading plan for your positions. This is particularly true for options trades, because unlike stocks, options have an expiry date. This expiry date means you are going to have to actively manage these positions due to the time decay that happens with options.

Last but not least, if you enjoyed reading this book and found it useful, I would very much appreciate if you took a few minutes to write a review on the Amazon website. The success of a book like this is based on honest reviews, and I will consider your comments in making future revisions. If you have any feedback, feel free to send me an email (brian@bearbulltraders.com).

Please remember that the author is NOT an investment advisory service, a registered investment advisor, or a broker-dealer. I do not undertake to advise clients or readers on which securities they should buy or sell for themselves. The information contained in this book is only a suggested starting point for doing additional independent research, in order to allow you to form your own opinions regarding trading and investments. It is suggested that investors and traders consult with their licensed financial advisors and tax advisors to determine the suitability of any investment.

Thank you for reading, and happy options trading!

Made in the USA
Monee, IL
16 December 2023

49462813R00098